American Sign Language Syntax

Approaches to Semiotics

52

MOUTON PUBLISHERS · THE HAGUE · PARIS · NEW YORK

American Sign Language Syntax

Scott K. Liddell
Department of Speech and Hearing Sciences
Indiana University,
Bloomington, Indiana

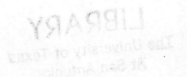

MOUTON PUBLISHERS · THE HAGUE · PARIS · NEW YORK

Library of Congress Cataloging in Publication Data

Liddell, Scott K   1946–
  American sign language syntax.

  (Approaches to semiotics; 52)
  Bibliography: p.
  Includes index.
  1. Deaf—Education—English language.   2. Sign
language.   3. English language—Syntax.   I. Title.
II. Series.
HV2469.E5L52   419   80–21374
ISBN 90–279–3437–1

ISBN: 90-279-3437-1
Jacket design by Jurriaan Schrofer
© 1980, Mouton Publishers, The Hague, The Netherlands
Printed in Great Britain

Preface

American Sign Language (ASL) is the sign language used by most of the deaf in the United States. ASL is distinct from sign systems which attempt to produce English manually. There are several such sign systems and they vary in the exactness with which they attempt to duplicate English. One of the least accurate ways of 'signing English' is to simply arrange signs in the same order they would appear in the English sentence which is being signed. Using a system like this, the 'Signed English' for 'The cat is sleeping on the fence', would be CAT SLEEP ON FENCE. Articles like 'a' or 'the', the plural marker 's', and suffixes like '-ed' and '-ing'. are not signed because ASL does not have signs for these English morphemes. This is not a reflection of a deficiency on the part of ASL, just a different organization of the grammar. The fact that ASL does not use articles, suffixes, etc., makes it similar to many languages of the world. Because the above 'Signed English' string does not contain equivalents for all the English forms, the 'Signed English' string is also the 'Signed English' for 'A cat is sleeping on a fence', 'A cat is sleeping on the fence', 'The cat slept on a fence', etc.

Other systems have been created in which signs for these missing parts were invented. One well-known system of this type is Signing Exact English (S.E.E.). Using a system like this it becomes possible to sign THE CAT IS SLEEP ING ON THE FENCE. This type of 'Signed English' system was designed to help the deaf student learn English. It also has benefits for hearing parents of deaf children. The parents can learn to communicate manually with their children by learning only lists of signs. They do not need to learn any new grammatical rules because they are not learning a new language, they are learning to produce the same language, English, on their hands. This is much easier than attempting to learn a new grammatical system. However, systems such as this have gone further than simply inventing signs for specific grammatical markers of English. A large number of S.E.E. signs are actually different in form from the corresponding ASL sign. That is, many existing signs have been 'initialized'. This means that the handshape for the sign has been changed to reflect the initial letter of the English word. For example, the ASL sign FRUSTRATED is made with a 5 handshape (flat hand but with the fingers spread apart). In S.E.E. signing the handshape for frustrated is an F handshape (like a 5 handshape but with the tip of the index finger and the tip of the thumb touching). In other cases, new signs were invented in this fashion when there were previously existing ASL signs for the same thing.

The term 'Signed English' refers to more than this, however. Some individuals also use the term to describe pidgins of ASL and English which incorporate grammatical aspects of both. For example, using such a pidgin, a signer could render the English 'I ran weekly' with the following mixture of ASL and English: 'PRO.1 RUN PAST WEEK++'. The notation '++' indicates a multiple repetition of the sign WEEK. The signs RUN and PAST are supposed to correspond to the English 'ran' (run + past). However, the repetition of the sign WEEK does not correspond to the English 'week + ly'. This repetition of the sign WEEK (which means 'weekly') is not a reflection of English morphology, but is part of a regular morphological process in ASL. In spite of this, there are some who would call this 'Signed English'. It should be clear that the term 'Signed English' is a very vague and potentially misleading term.

None of these systems (or pidgins) is being studied here. This study is based on ASL as used by deaf signers of deaf parents when communicating with one another. When communicating with hearing persons, the deaf signer is likely to use some form of 'Signed English'. This is the language of the classroom and also the 'prestige' language. Further, the hearing person is not likely to know much about ASL, at least not as much as he knows about 'Signed English'. As a result, the deaf signer does not expect the average hearing signer to understand ASL and would therefore use 'Signed English', which he does expect the hearing signer to understand.

As a result, pure ASL data can be difficult to come by. It is always possible for 'Signed English' data to slip in. The deaf native signers who provided the data used in this dissertation are aware of the potential difficulty and have carefully reviewed the data presented here in discussions and seminars. In all cases, I have relied on the intuitions of deaf native signers (i.e. signers who learned ASL from their deaf parents). It is hoped that in this way, the data will be as genuine a reflection of ASL as possible.

Acknowledgements

This study would never have been completed were it not for the help and encouragement of several people. I owe a great debt to Edward S. Klima, whose contributions of time, effort, and great insight have been invaluable. The assistance and support of Ursula Bellugi has also been of great value. Nearly all of the research reported in this study was carried out in her research laboratory at the Salk Institute for Biological Studies. Other colleagues and friends who have had an influence on the clarification of the ideas presented in this study are Charlotte Baker, Robbin Battison, Sandra Chung, S.-Y. Kuroda, Ronald W. Langacker, William Mathews, William Nagy, Don Newkirk, Elissa Newport, Kunihiko Ogawa, Carlene Pedersen, Nancy Stensen, and Ted Supalla.

I owe a great debt to those who taught me American Sign Language. Sharon Neumann Solow got me interested in studying ASL and got me started through an introductory course taught by her. Carlene Canady Pedersen provided most of the initial data used in my research and taught me most of the ASL that I know. She has responded patiently to seemingly endless questioning and, because of her willingness to examine carefully her intuitions about the subtleties of ASL, has been an invaluable source of information. Bonnie Gough, Sandra Hafer, and Ted Supalla have also been very helpful and willing to share their native intuitions about ASL.

Ray Jones and Harry Murphy from the Center on Deafness at California State University, Northridge, have been very cooperative in arranging for some of my ASL research to be done at CSUN. I would like to thank all the students who volunteered to participate in the research conducted there.

I would also like to thank Gilbert Eastman for telling me about and providing me with a very interesting excerpt from the book, *The Life of Thomas Hopkins Gallaudet.*

Carlene Canady Pedersen has graciously consented to serve as a model for all the photographic illustrations of the nonmanual behaviors discussed here. The drawings were done by Frank Paul.

Financial support has come from the University of California, San Diego, in the form of a fellowship and a research grant. This work was also supported in part by National Institute of Health grant No. NS–09811 to the Salk Institute for Biological Studies and National Science Foundation grant No. BNS–76–12866 to the Salk Institute for Biological Studies.

Finally, I would like to thank my wife, Skuntala, for her patience and support.

Contents

List of Illustrations

Abbreviations and Glossing Conventions

The following conventions will be used for the English translation gloss of American Sign Language (ASL) utterances. Individual
signs will be written in small capital letters (e.g. EUROPE). When
more than one word is required to translate a single sign, the
words will be connected with hyphens (e.g. LONG-AGO). If two
signs are signed as a compound, the two signs will be connected
with a superscript arc (e.g. FEEL͡LIKE).

Free English translations of ASL sentences are written in quotes
with standard English capitalization. Reference to the first-person
singular is made by pointing to the center of the chest with the
index finger. All such references will be transcribed PRO.1. Reference to the first person plural will be transcribed PRO.1pl. The
same will apply to the pronoun SELF (e.g. SELF.2 = 'yourself')
and the possessive marker POSS (e.g. POSS.3 - 'its', 'his', or 'hers').

When a verb indicates its subject because of its movement,
location, or orientation with respect to a given index (location in
space), that subject will be shown in raised brackets preceding the
sign, using an 'X' to indicate reference to an index and lower case
pronominal notation to identify that index. An object will be
shown in raised brackets following the sign

(e.g. $^{[X:\ pro.3]}$GIVE$^{[X:\ pro.1]}$ = 'he gave me'). If a verb is inflected

for aspect, raised brackets will also be used. The notation 'I' will
indicate an inflection of the sign and will be followed by the

type of inflection (e.g. DRIVE$^{[I:\ continuous]}$ indicates that the sign

DRIVE has been inflected for continuous aspect. To indicate the modulation or inflection of a sign without specifically identifying it, I will use the notation '+' inside the raised brackets (e.g. EAT[+], indicates that the sign EAT is not made in citation form).

If a nonmanual signal 'Y' (i.e. a specific facial expression, head position or movement, or body position or movement, or a specific combination of these) occurs throughout a sign sequence such

as DOG CHASE CAT, this will be symbolized by $\overline{\text{DOG CHASE CAT}}^{\text{Y}}$.

The following notation will indicate that a sign is made and then held: BOY——————. The line extending from the sign indicates the duration of the hold. If a sign is made and held with one hand, and then another sign is made with the other hand, this

will be indicated in the following way: BOY——————.
PRO.3

This indicates that the sign BOY was made first, then held while the sign PRO.3 was made.

Background

1.0. INTRODUCTION

ASL has been called a manual–visual language because (presumably) it is produced by the hands and perceived by the eyes. However, one of the early findings of this work was that there are many cases where facial expression, head position and movement, and body position and movement are significant in forming signals which carry *linguistic* information necessary for an understanding of the structure of ASL utterances. The importance of this nonmanual activity can be appreciated when it is seen that neither word order, subordination, nor relativization can be discussed in depth without reference to nonmanual signals.

First we will briefly review most of the work which has been done on the functions of facial expression, head position, body position, etc., in ASL discourse. Section 1.4 outlines the topics to be covered in this book.

1.1. NONMANUAL SIGNALS

1.1.0. *Introduction*

In an 1888 publication, *The Life of Thomas Hopkins Gallaudet*, it is reported that Gallaudet experimented with the face as a possible vehicle for a spelling system.[1] In this system the expression of awe would denote the letter 'a'; boldness – the letter 'b'; curiosity – the letter 'c'; despair – the letter 'd'; eagerness – the letter 'e'; fear — the letter 'f'; and so on. Thus the word 'deaf' could be spelled by consecutive facial expressions of despair, eagerness, awe, and fear. Fortunately for the deaf, the experiment was abandoned. However, it does reveal Gallaudet's awareness of the potential importance of the face as a message-carrying medium.

The first published reference to the use of nonmanual signals in ASL that I have been able to find comes from *American Annals of the Deaf*, in an 1872 article by E. G. Valentine. In that article Valentine quotes the Rev. T. H. Gallaudet as having said, 'A teacher of deaf-mutes cannot be thoroughly qualified for his profession without being master of the language of signs — *natural*, as expressed by the countenance, gestures and attitudes of the body; and *artificial*, as far as art has enlarged and perfected this natural language'. As should be clear from this passage, published more than a century ago, educators of the deaf were aware that signers did more than produce signs with their hands. Their faces were active rather than relaxed, and the body itself was apparently also significant. Anyone observing ASL could make the same comments today.

One of the aims of this book will be to examine nonmanual signals and to determine what role, if any, they play in the grammatical structure of the language. That is, there are many possible functions that these nonmanual activities could be performing. They might be involved in word formation — a lexical function. They might be important in sentence formation — a syntactic function. They might also be found to function like tone of voice in spoken language — a communicative but not a grammatical function.

1.1.1. Nonmanual signals used as grammatical markers

1.1.1.1. Yes–no questions. It has often been observed that nonmanual activity is used in forming yes–no questions in ASL. This has been discussed in Stokoe et al. (1965), Bellugi and Fischer (1972), Baker (1976a, 1976b), and others. All these agree that a particular facial expression, head position, and body position signals the yes–no question. The nature of this nonmanual signal is illustrated in Plate 1.

The face and body are forward and the brows are raised during

$$\overline{\hspace{8cm}}^{\text{q}}$$
WOMAN   FORGET   PURSE

Plate 1.

the signs WOMAN, FORGET, and PURSE. This will be transcribed as
$\overline{\text{WOMAN FORGET PURSE}}^{\text{q}}$. The continuous line above these signs represents the duration of the yes–no question signal. The 'q' at the
end of the line represents the particular type of signalling activity
represented by the line above the signs.

Without the nonmanual signal which accompanies the three
signs, the sequence would not be interpreted as a yes–no question.
It is important to mention here that the string is not well formed
if the nonmanual signal accompanies only part of the question.
For this reason the sequence $\overline{\text{WOMAN FORGET}}^{\text{q}}$ PURSE is not a
well-formed question.

This aspect of the nonmanual grammatical signals, that the
duration of the nonmanual signals is strictly correlated with the
manual signs, is one which has not been sufficiently emphasized
by those who have discussed nonmanual signals; but the regular
interrelationship between the nonmanual signals and the manual
signs will be of crucial importance here.

1.1.1.2. Headshake negation. Another function of nonmanual
signals which has been described by Stokoe (1960), Bellugi and
Fischer (1972), and Baker (1976a, 1976b), consists of a side-to-
side headshake accompanied by a nonneutral facial expression
which, without any lexical help, negates a sentence. A facial

expression which, if combined with a side-to-side headshake, will form a negating signal is illustrated in Plate 2.

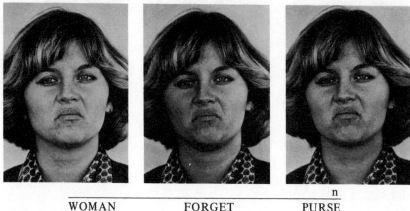

		n
WOMAN	FORGET	PURSE

Plate 2.

The same three signs, WOMAN, FORGET, and PURSE, are used in this example; however, because of the accompanying nonmanual signal, the sentence is interpreted as 'It is not the case that the woman forgot her purse'. If the sentence which this signal accompanies is lexically negated, WOMAN NOT FORGET PURSE, and accompanied by the nonmanual negation signal above, the accompanying nonmanual negation signal will not change the polarity of the sentence but will reinforce the negativity of the sentence.

According to Bellugi and Fischer (1972) and Baker (1976a, 1976b), frowning and lowering the brows also constitutes a negating signal.

1.1.1.3. Topicalization. Fischer (1975) also alluded to nonmanual signals in describing topicalized elements in ASL. She claims that a sentence containing a topicalized element will have an 'intonation break' between the topicalized constituent and the rest of the sentence, 'accomplished by pauses, head tilts, raising of the eyebrows, and/or probably numerous other cues that I as a nonnative, nondeaf signer have yet to learn to pay attention to' (1975: 6). This is an example where a change in word order (e.g. topicalizing an object) is reflected nonmanually. Exactly what the nonmanual signalling consists of will be discussed in Chapter 2. How this relates to the question of 'basic word order' in ASL will be discussed in Chapter 3.

Baker (1976a, 1976b) also describes the use of other non-manual signals in connection with conditional sentences. She reports that in a small set of data she found that if the if-clause proposition was contrary to fact, the brows would be lowered at the beginning of the clause. If the if-clause proposition was a real-world possibility, the brows were raised at the beginning of the clause. This type of construction will not be examined here.

1.1.2. Other uses of nonmanual signals

Baker (1976a, 1976b) gives examples of nonmanual signals performing modifying functions. She gives an example of non-manual activity which can accompany the sign TREE and result in the meaning, 'big tree'. Before the sign TREE is made, the eyes look right and the head tilts back, then as the sign TREE is being made (above the citation level), the eyes widen and are directed toward the fingertips, and the cheeks puff up. Then the head tilts further back, the shoulders raise, and the sign TREE itself continues rising. This type of nonmanual activity will also not be examined.

1.1.3. Referential uses of nonmanual activity

1.1.3.1. Eye gaze. There are several descriptions of nonmanual activities that have referential functions; Fischer (1975), Friedman (1976), Bendixen (1975), and Baker (1976a, 1976b) all make reference to nonmanual activities with this function. There are two basic types of activity that are described. The first is the use of eye gaze. A common process in ASL is the association of a noun and a location in space. Once an association is established between a location in space and a nominal argument (i.e. JOHN), reference to that location is functionally equivalent to pronominal reference in spoken language. Both Bendixen (1975) and Baker (1976a, 1976b) discuss eye gaze and its use in this process. Both report that the eyes are directed initially toward the location to be established, apparently a normal part of the location-establishment process. Baker also reports that eye gaze alone can also be used to refer to an established argument.

1.1.3.2. Body orientation. A second referential use of nonmanual activity is hinted at in Fischer (1975) and discussed in more detail in Friedman (1976). This involves shifting the orientation of the body to 'take on' one or more third person 'roles' (Friedman 1976: 132). That is, suppose a location for someone has been established on the signer's right. By turning his own body or head to the left, the signer can take on the role of the person who was established on the right. If the signer then signs PRO.1, since he has taken on the role of the referent established on the right, the signer no longer refers to himself as the signer but to the self which was established on the right. We will see in Chapter 2 that role playing can also be accomplished without the establishment of spatial loci.

1.1.4. Turn taking in ASL discourse

Baker (1976) reports that eye gaze plays an important part in the turn-taking process in ASL. I will not present a comprehensive review of her findings here, but the process she describes turns on a very basic fact about communication: You can't communicate with me if I'm not listening to you. For the hearing person, it is very difficult not to hear the words that someone else is saying to you. Some piece of apparatus would be required to drown out the other person's speech signal. Earphones and loud music would do the trick. With the deaf, however, by simply turning the head and eyes away, the speaker – addressee link is broken. Baker discovered that *speakers* make use of this fact. That is, you can only be interrupted if you are looking at the person who wants to interrupt. She found that speakers, especially if there is competition for the floor, spend a large percentage of their signing time not looking at the addressee. This use of nonmanual behaviors for regulating conversations will not be discussed.

1.1.5. Universal facial activity

More than 100 years ago Charles Darwin made the claim that some facial expressions are innately determined and are the same across cultures. His work was rejected at the time because of his emphasis on innate determinants. However, now, more than 100 years after Darwin's original work, the sameness across cultures has been demonstrated (Ekman and Friesen 1975).

Ekman and Friesen claim that for at least six emotions — surprise, fear, disgust, anger, happiness, and sadness — the facial appearance is universal, though there may be cultural differences as to when these facial expressions are shown (1975: 23).

If these expressions are indeed universal, as they appear to be, then we would expect signers to use them. Chapter 2 will explore the way signers use at least some of these expressions.

1.2. WORD ORDER

1.2.1. Fischer on word order

Fischer (1975) claims that ASL is basically a subject–verb–object language. By this she does not mean that every sentence in ASL will use SVO order. Rather, this means that this is the order one finds if there have been no changes of the original underlying SVO order. Fischer claimed that any changes in the SVO order would be reflected by 'intonation breaks' (accomplished by pauses, head tilts, raising of the eyebrows, and/or probably numerous other cues) (1975: 6). The following illustrates the word orders she discusses and the 'intonation breaks' associated with them.

NVN   This is the underlying order. The initial noun is the subject and the final noun is the object. There are no breaks.

N,NV   The object has been topicalized and there is a break between it and the rest of the sentence. The result is an O,SV order.

VN,N   The verb phrase has been topicalized and there is a break between it and the rest of the sentence. Fischer also claims that this order could be a result of the postposition of the subject rather than the topicalization of the verb phrase.

Fischer also claimed that word order was considerably freer if there was no possibility of confusion based on the semantics of the lexical items in a sentence. She points out that this freedom of word order is not possible where there could be ambiguity as to which noun is the subject and which is the object. She also claimed that SOV order could also be used if the verb, by its direction or orientation, indicated its subject and object. This will be discussed in more detail in Chapter 3.

1.2.2. Friedman on word order

Friedman (1976) also observes that several word orders occur. However, she denies that there is any grammatical significance to the different orders. Her attempt to justify this claim will be discussed in detail in Chapter 3.

1.3. SUBORDINATION

Fischer (1974) notes that in ASL the so-called function words are absent. This includes markers of subordination. However, this does not mean that ASL has no subordinate structure, and Fischer presents a number of sentences which she analyzes as containing complements of verbs such as THINK and DENY. She also discusses auxiliaries which she claims function as higher verbs: MUST, FINISH, HAPPEN, BETTER, and SUCCEED. She also demonstrates that sentences containing what appear to be complement clauses do have structure as shown by the intonation patterns which occur. (Recall that in general by 'intonation patterns' she means nonmanual signals as well as timing or rhythm, though here she does not specify what nonmanual signal(s) she is referring to or whether she means rhythm only.)

Thompson (1977) makes the tentative claim that there is no syntactic subordination in ASL. He was led to this claim by his failure to find relative clauses in ASL (cf. Chapter 5 for a description of one type of relative-clause structure in ASL). He then examines a number of constructions which are reasonable candidates for subordination and concludes that they are not cases involving subordination. He analyzes them as being either coordinate or conjoined in some way. The train of thought which led him to this conclusion will be examined in detail in Chapter 4.

1.4. THE ORGANIZATION OF THIS BOOK

To a great extent, determining the structure of ASL utterances depends not only on the signs that are produced but also on other things which don't generally find their way into linguistic trees. As the reader has seen, this includes the expression on the signer's face, his eye gaze, the orientation of his head, the movement of his head, the orientation of his body, and the movement of his body.

Chapter 2 will discuss nonmanual signals and their various roles in the linguistic and paralinguistic structure of ASL. There will be no attempt to analyze every nonmanual signalling behavior which has been observed. Rather, typical instances of certain types of nonmanual signals will be analyzed. Several problems will also be raised and left unsolved.

Chapter 3 argues for the underlying subject–verb–object nature of ASL. The argumentation depends heavily on the use of nonmanual signals. This chapter will also examine the use of classifiers in ASL and their effect on word order. Finally, Fischer's analysis of the historical change from subject–object–verb order to subject–verb–object order will be examined and a new analysis of this change will be presented.

Chapter 4 reviews Thompson (1977) in detail and presents evidence from several directions which supports the existence of subordination in ASL.

Chapter 5 presents an analysis of a major form of subordination in ASL — relative clauses. Once again, the analysis depends heavily on the use of nonmanual signals.

NOTES

1. ASL has its origins in France, where the Abbé Charles Michel de l'Epée formalized French Sign Language in the latter part of the eighteenth century. In 1816 Laurent Clerc, a deaf Frenchman, accompanied the Reverend Thomas Hopkins Gallaudet, an American, to the United States to help establish a school for the deaf. The two came to America in 1816 and established the first school for the deaf in the United States. It was located in Hartford, Connecticut, and called the American Asylum for the Deaf and Dumb (now the American School for the Deaf). For more details the reader is referred to Frishberg (1975).

2

Nonmanual Signals

2.0. INTRODUCTION

An obvious fact about humans is that they communicate with each other in many ways. One way that people can communicate, if they know the same language, is by speaking that language. However, if they don't know the same language, they must try to communicate in some other way. For example, they could point to things, pictures, etc. They could try to act out some situation: a hungry traveler could pretend to be eating, then point to his stomach with a distressed look on his face to communicate to someone that he was looking for a place to eat.

Even speakers of the same language often use gestures instead of words to communicate. For example if one person saw that someone else was having difficulty parking a car parallel to the curb because the space was small, the good Samaritan, being unafraid of a later lawsuit, could indicate the distance between the two cars by placing his own hands that distance apart. He could even bring his hands closer together as the cars got closer together. The message would be clearly understood.

Other types of actions are also communicative. Consider, for example, the "courtship dance" of the American adolescent. Birdwhistell (1970) reports that the Interdisciplinary Committee on Culture and Communication at the University of Louisville found it quite easy to identify some twenty-four steps in this 'dance'.

For example, if a boy takes a girl's hand, he must await a counterpressure on his hand before beginning the finger-intertwine.

This takes place, ideally, before he casually and tentatively puts his arm around her shoulders.

The study also found that a person was not judged as 'fast' if (s)he went quickly through the steps. Rather, a person was called 'fast' if (s)he skipped steps or reversed their order (Birdwhistell 1970: 159). Clearly, the actions in the 'courtship dance' are also communicative.

People also communicate their feelings by the expressions on their faces. In fact, the facial expressions for the emotional states of surprise, anger, happiness, fear, sadness, and disgust are claimed to be universal by Ekman and Friesen (1975). Of course, there are also many other messages that can be sent by the face.

The point is that there are many ways of communicating that are quite independent of what is traditionally called 'language', and what linguists analyze as language. I will assume that there is some justification for making a distinction between language and other means of communication and note that, if the language under consideration is a spoken language, the object of linguistic study will be a subset of what is produced by the vocal apparatus; excluding, for example, things like intentionally clearing the throat to communicate disapproval or to attract attention.

Even where there is agreement that something is 'part of the language' and involved in the sentence production process, there can be disagreement as to whether or not it plays a syntactic role. A case in point is intonation in spoken language.

Though some linguists study intonation, it is not generally analyzed as part of the syntactic structure of an utterance. For example, in discussing a group of phenomena referred to as prosody or suprasegmentals, Bolinger (1975: 46) says the following: 'They are a kind of musical accompaniment to speech, just as gesture is a kind of histrionic accompaniment' (p. 46).

However, at least two types of suprasegmentals appear to perform syntactic functions. These are what have been called 'question intonation' and 'contrastive stress'. 'Question intonation' is the sole marker distinguishing the question (2) from the assertion (1):

(1)   You are going to run tomorrow.
(2)   You are going to run tomorrow?

Similarly, certain changes in loudness and pitch can make a

difference in identifying the referent of a pronoun. Consider the following two sentences:

(3)   John *kicked* Bill and then he *hit* Sally.
(4)   John kicked *Bill* and then *he* hit Sally.

The italicized words above might be said to have 'contrastive stress' (though the entire intonation patterns of the two sentences appear to be different).

In (3) 'he' refers to John, while in (4) 'he' refers to Bill. The meanings of the two strings are markedly different even though they both contain exactly the same words. If a separate word established who did what to whom in these two examples, a syntactician would include that word as part of the syntactic structure of the utterance. Yet here, where the same function is carried out by 'intonation', the 'intonation' will probably not find its way into the syntactic structure of the utterance. Consider the following from Bolinger (1975: 49): 'As many yes–no questions in English go down in pitch as go up. The ones that go up are those in which the speaker is genuinely curious. Rising intonation is often cited as one grammatical mark of a yes–no question, but it is more truly gestural, like raised eyebrows'.

Similarly in ASL, the dividing line between what constitutes the language signal and what is merely communicative is unclear. Also for those things that are considered to be 'part of the language' and involved in the process of sentence formation, the distinction between those things with syntactic function and those with no syntactic function is also not always clear.

Someone might argue that what the signer does with his hands should serve as the raw data for linguistic analysis, and that what he does with his face, head, and body are paralinguistic (parallel to the way that intonation as well as gestures which accompany spoken language have been analyzed). I would like to suggest in this chapter that that kind of arbitrary division won't work.

When I first began studying ASL, it was not obvious that nonmanual activity played any role in syntax, semantics, the lexicon, etc. As a result, my first efforts were directed solely at analyzing the signs themselves. This did not turn out to be a productive approach. It is possible, for example, to indicate that a dog chased a cat with the signs DOG, CHASE, and CAT ordered in any of the following ways:

(5)   DOG CHASE CAT
       DOG CAT CHASE
       CAT DOG CHASE
       CHASE CAT DOG

The following two orders do not occur with the intended relationship between the dog and the cat:

(6)   CHASE DOG CAT
       CAT CHASE DOG

Many investigators have noticed that ASL can indicate the relationships between subject and object by the direction and/or orientation of the verb, yet in the acceptable sequences in (5) this directional property of verbs was not always used.

I decided to look at other things the signers were doing, their use of facial expression, head position, body position, etc., to see if these activities might shed some light on the interpretation of ASL sentences — and more specifically on the interplay between the manual signs themselves and certain nonmanual gestures that appeared with the manual signs in patterned ways.

People seeing ASL for the first time are immediately struck by a signer's seemingly continuous use of rapidly changing facial expressions. A signer's face is rarely 'neutral' or relaxed; signing is also accompanied by 'nonneutral' head position, head movements, and body movements.

When a hearing daughter of deaf parents, who had learned ASL as a native language and thus was fluent in both ASL and English, was asked to tell a specific story in both languages, she used a lot of facial expression, head movement and body movement in the ASL version but almost no facial or body activity in the spoken-English version. Even when we compare an individual signer's use of nonmanual activity in ASL with his use in Signed English, another *gesture* language he knows well, we find that a given signer will use much more nonmanual activity in ASL.

Such informal observations suggest that the nonmanual activity which occurs in ASL discourse is not simply a function of individual expressiveness on the signer's part; nor is it characteristic of *any* manual language a signer might use, fingerspelling, for example; rather, it evidently performs functions specific to ASL.

In the pages that follow I will try to distinguish between activities with 'linguistic function' and those with 'communicative function'. The distinction will not be made on the basis of how a signal is articulated, but rather on whether a *linguistic* function can be demonstrated.

The nonmanual behaviors discussed in this chapter are made up of specific contractions of facial muscles, combined with head movements or positions and body movements or positions. They were gathered from videotaped narratives as well as elicited from signers.

These nonmanual behaviors range from movements of the face in pantomime (where, it should be added, signers' intuitions generally agree in characterizing this as not 'signing' in the narrow sense) to specific nonmanual signals which are obligatory in specific syntactic structures.

Between these two extremes there is a large range of nonmanual behaviors, including some that hearing nonsigners use. In all cases I have attempted to uncover a relationship between the non-manual behavior and the manually produced signs that could be considered diagnostic of the level of communication structure at which the nonmanual behaviors are operating. Some of these non-manual behaviors seemed to play a role in the syntactic structure of the ASL utterances, while for others no such role was found.

Some of the nonmanual behaviors were obviously emblems shared by the American speech community and some of them were apparently universal (dropping the jaw and widening the eyes to indicate surprise, for example; cf. Ekman and Friesen 1975).

The fact that a certain type of nonmanual behavior was shared by others outside the ASL community did not result in its being disregarded as nonlinguistic. I left open the possibility that it might nonetheless have a linguistic function in ASL. That is, it might still be possible that these behaviors which are not restric-ted to an ASL context might interact in a special way with the syntactic and lexical structure of ASL.

2.0.1. Data gathering

The data concerning the use of nonmanual signals in ASL were gathered during a three-year period in the form of signed narratives or shorter signed utterances elicited from deaf native signers (i.e. a deaf ASL signer whose parents are also deaf ASL signers). The signing produced is video-taped and a native signer later translates from the video-tape in as much detail as possible. Other signers' translations are used for confirmation.

The videotape records 60 images per second. Each of these images is called a field. It is possible to view these fields individually, thereby freezing the action taking place at the time. The data involving nonmanual activity are analyzed field by field so that the exact beginning and end of the nonmanual behavior can be located. This is a very important part of the data, since not only is the presence of a signal during a sign sequence important, but the duration and exact location of the signal in time is also very important. As we will see later, the onset of a particular nonmanual behavior can make a significant difference in the interpretation of the ASL. As was mentioned earlier, it can also make the difference between a grammatical and an ungrammatical sequence. That is, in some cases the nonmanual signal must be coterminous with the manual signs in a given string.

Most of the data was gathered using two videotape cameras. One was focused on the signer from the waist up including the head, and the other was focused entirely on the signer's face. By using a special-effects generator, it was possible to cover most of the television screen with the signer's face and insert the view of the signer from the waist up in the lower right-hand corner. This made possible a close-up look at the face and simultaneous reference to the signs that were being made at the same time.

In many cases photographs were taken of the screen as every sign was being made, and proof sheets of the 35-mm negatives were made and cut into strips. A gloss for each sign was then placed underneath the picture of the sign that was being made at that time. This technique turned out to be particularly useful since it presents a permanent image of the facial expression, the position of the head, etc. Trying to recall what one facial expression looked like while looking at another expression proved to be nearly impossible. Having a permanent image of a given expression made comparison of one signer's expressions quite easy, and also made it possible to compare facial expressions across signers.

One problem which faces anyone attempting to describe nonmanual activities in ASL is that no two occurrences of a particular nonmanual activity will be exactly the same (naturally this is also true for the production of signs or the pronunciation of words). This would be true even if a signer was attempting to recreate exactly the same muscular activity time after time. However, even this is not true of signers. There may be times when a signer wishes to articulate very carefully (both manually and non-manually), and other times when the signer does not wish to be so careful. In these cases even the muscular 'target' is not the same. As a result there is a range through which a particular nonmanual signalling activity can acceptably vary. For the most part there will be no attempt to set limits on the range of variation possible for each nonmanual activity described. Rather, for each nonmanual signal to be discussed, the prototypical form will be described.

2.1. NONMANUAL ACTIVITY IN THE LEXICAL SYSTEM

Certain nonmanual behaviors (and in particular, specific manipulation of the facial muscles) in ASL are associated specifically with particular lexical items. In such cases I have observed that the behavior is coterminous with the manual sign. The sign BITE is often accompanied by a biting motion of the mouth, BEG by a pleading expression, RELIEVED by a rapid exhaling of a burst of air through pursed lips (almost like 'phew!'). The nonmanual behaviors above appear to serve the function of acting out the meaning of the sign in some way, though this is not true for all nonmanual behaviors which appear to be operating at the lexical level. The sign GIVE-IN is often accompanied by dropping the jaw and occasionally even vocal articulations like '[ba]' (Robbin Battison, personal communication). In this case I see no evidence for a pantomimic connection between the sign GIVE-IN and the accompanying nonmanual activity.

One might regard these nonmanual behaviors as a type of optional reinforcer of the manual sign, which would provide some redundancy in the language signal. Whether or not these types of movement should be regarded as part of the citation form of the sign or a usual addition to it is a difficult question; of the signs above Stokoe et al. (1965) list only RELIEVED as being made optionally with a sigh. However, since some signers consistently use facial-muscle and other nonmanual activity when asked to produce these signs in citation form, the question remains open.

One argument in favor of regarding this nonmanual activity as part of the lexical item itself is that the nonmanual activity can be present even if the lexical item is negated. This is seen in the following example.

(7) NOT WORRY. DOG NOT BITE $^{[X:\ pro.3]}$.
'Don't worry. The dog didn't bite him.'

Even in this negative case the signer could accompany the sign BITE $^{[X:\ pro.3]}$ with the biting motion discussed above.

This same use of nonmanual activity actually appears to distinguish some otherwise formationally identical signs. A sign made like SUNRISE but with an F handshape and coterminous with a particular nonmanual signal is interpreted to mean 'oversleep'. With another specific nonmanual signal the interpretation is 'sleep in' (Ted Supalla brought the 'sleep in' example to my attention).

It appears that a particular facial expression and headshake are so strongly associated with the sign NOT-YET that the manual sign can be omitted from a string, as long as the nonmanual activity is present in its place. For example, to indicate that he had not eaten yet, a signer could say, PRO.1 NOT-YET EAT (with the appropriate facial expression and headshake with the sign NOT-YET). Alternatively, he could forego using his hands in signing NOT-YET while keeping the nonmanual signals in the same place (between PRO.1 and EAT), and the interpretation would be the same. The form of facial expression associated with NOT-YET is shown in Plate 3.

Frishberg (1975) has found evidence for a historical shift away from the use of nonmanual activities in the citation form of ASL signs toward a concentration of lexical information in the hands. This is interpreted by her as part of a general shift in ASL from iconicity in signs to arbitrariness. She has found signs which previously required facial expression, environmental contact, or body movement, and now only require movement of the hands.

The following example is typical:

COMPARE is one of the few signs for which we have information from OFSL [Old French Sign Language], as well as from Long and Stokoe, et al. The original form of this sign had two flat hands facing the signer, separated. The eyes moved from one to the other, and then the hands moved together, eyes focused on both at once. Long describes an intermediate stage in which the hands have begun moving 'inward and up before you side by side as if looking at them and comparing palms' (99). The modern form simply rocks the two hands, either in alternation (which can be related to the older eye movements) or in unison — an arbitrary, but symmetrical change (Frishberg 1975: 711).

NOT-YET

Plate 3.

There is no reason to suppose that this process will not continue. However, for the present, there are still many signs which are typically signed with a specific facial expression or body movement.

2.2   NONMANUAL GRAMMATICAL MARKERS

2.2.0. Introduction

While facial expression in ASL — information communicated in a channel entirely different from the 'major' channel of articulation — may be on the wane in its use as part of lexical items, its function as a marker of abstract grammatical distinctions is very much alive. One such marker can mark a string as a question rather than an assertion (to the same extent that the rising intonation marks English yes–no questions in which the subject and auxiliary have not been reversed). This nonmanual signal is most often the sole marker for the yes–no question.

Another nonmanual signal can mark a sign sequence as a restrictive relative clause rather than an independent clause, and another can mark a sign or phrase as the topic of a sentence (Chapter 5 examines relative clauses in detail).

The use of these grammatical markers can be simply illustrated. The three-sign sequence WOMAN FORGET PURSE can have any of the following interpretations depending solely on the nonmanual grammatical markers which accompany the signs:

(8)   'The woman forgot the purse.' (no special marker)

(9)   'Did the woman forget the purse?' (yes–no question marker)

(10) 'The woman who forgot the purse . . . ' (relative clause marker)

(11) 'As for the woman, (she) forgot the purse.' (topic marker)

2.2.1. Neutral statements

Plate 4 illustrates the simple sentence WOMAN FORGET PURSE: 'The woman forgot the purse.'[1]

WOMAN   FORGET   PURSE

Plate 4.

2.2.2. Yes–no questions

Plate 5 illustrates the same three signs in the same order but

$$\overline{\hspace{5cm}}^{\,q}$$
WOMAN   FORGET   PURSE

Plate 5.

accompanied by a nonmanual signal which marks yes–no questions:
the head and shoulders are leaned forward, the chin is forward
far enough to keep the face relatively vertical and the eyebrows
are raised. This signal, which is discussed in Stokoe et al. (1965),
identifies the sign sequence as a yes–no question.

$$\overline{\hspace{4.5cm}}^{\,q}$$
(12)   WOMAN FORGET PURSE
      'Did the woman forget the purse?'

A bar above a sign or sign sequence will be used to represent
the presence and duration of a specific nonmanual signal. In
this case the bar represents the signer's use of a particular combination of activities involving the eyebrows, the head, and
the body in forming the yes–no question signal described above.
The letter or letters at the end of the bar represent the particular
type of nonmanual activity which was present throughout the
sign or sequence of signs underneath the bar. In this case 'q'
symbolizes the presence of these three nonmanual behaviors:

$$\begin{bmatrix} \text{brow raise} \\ \text{head forward} \\ \text{body forward} \end{bmatrix}$$

We will see later that the brow raise will also occur as part of other
nonmanual signals. I should also note that while the fullest form
of the question signal consists of all three nonmanual components, sometimes a brow raise alone is sufficient to signal a
yes–no question.

ASL can also mark yes–no questions manually, with a sign made by the finger drawing a question mark and adding a dot with a stab (Gᵊ⊥) (Stokoe et al. 1965: 65).² This sign does not replace the nonmanual signal but is used in conjunction with it. Without the facial expression, the same sign may be used to express doubt or disagreement.

This same sign and a variant [an index finger erect at the base but bending repeatedly at the first two joints, the palm oriented toward the addressee] have another use, as a one-sign utterance expressing slight skepticism, doubt, or polite but complete disagreement about another's statement. Curiously the 'question mark' sign *with appropriate facial expression* works at either end of the range: 'Oh, do you think so?' and 'I question that very much' (Stokoe et al. 1965: 65; emphasis added).

It appears to be the case that facial expression and body movement play the determining role in the identification of yes–no questions in ASL since (1) the facial expression and body attitude alone can signal a yes–no question but signs alone will not, and (2) the interpretation of the two 'question signs' depends on facial expression and body movement.

2.2.3. Restrictive relative clauses

It should be obvious by now that without attending to nonmanual signals, it is possible for the analyst to miss significant linguistic processes in the language. It has been claimed, for example, that ASL exhibits no syntactic subordination of any kind (Thompson 1977). But when, for instance, the same sequence of signs WOMAN FORGET PURSE is produced with the nonmanual signal illustrated in Plate 6 and symbolized by 'r', we shall argue that the sign sequence forms a restrictive relative clause: 'The woman who forgot her purse . . . . ' Such a relative clause may function as the subject of a sentence, as in:

(13)   <u>WOMAN FORGET PURSE</u> RECENTLY ARRIVE
       'The woman who forgot the purse just arrived.'

The relative-clause portion of this complex sentence is illustrated in Plate 6.

                                         r

WOMAN   FORGET   PURSE

Plate 6.

This type of relative clause is discussed in detail in Chapter 5. The nonmanual behaviors which form this signal are the following:

$$\begin{bmatrix} \text{brow raise} \\ \text{head tilted back} \\ \text{upper lip raised} \end{bmatrix}$$

There is no difference in the way the brows are raised in this signal and the way the brows are raised in the yes–no question.

2.2.4. Topics

Nonmanual signals are also involved in distinguishing the topic of a sentence from a nontopic. Plate 7 illustrates the string WOMAN FORGET PURSE with the first sign, WOMAN, marked as a topic. We are using the word 'topic' here in the sense of old information about which some comment will be made. Topics are accompanied by a slight backward head tilt and a brow raise. Again, there is no distinction between the brow raise used in this signal and the brow raise in yes–no questions and relative clauses. We will symbolize the presence of these two nonmanual behaviors by 't'.

$$\text{'t'} = \begin{bmatrix} \text{brow raise} \\ \\ \text{slight backward head tilt} \end{bmatrix}$$

In addition, topics are held longer than nontopics.

There is quite a bit of variation in exactly how long a given sign is held. Among the variables which affect the length of a sign

t
WOMAN   FORGET   PURSE

Plate 7.

is whether or not the sign is accompanied by the nonmanual signal 't'. I have found that sentence-initial signs which are accompanied by the signal 't' are held roughly one-fifth of a second longer than sentence-initial signs which are not accompanied by the 't' signal.[3]

In this section we have looked at three different grammatical markers in ASL. Their grammatical function is obvious, and there can be no question that these three signals are clearly part of the language signal in ASL. In the next section we will look at several types of head movements which occur during ASL signing and attempt to distinguish between those that are linguistic and those that are communicative but not so clearly linguistic.

2.3. HEAD NODS AND HEADSHAKES

2.3.1. Head nods with communicative function

2.3.1.0. Introduction. Birdwhistell (1970) discusses the use of head nods by interviewers. He found three distinct types of head nods that interviewers used while the person being interviewed was talking. The first was a single head nod ('n'). He found that this nod seems to sustain interaction without a significant change in the level or content of the communication. A double head nod ('nn'), which is distinct in form from two single head nods, was seen to stimulate elaboration by the person being interviewed. A form consisting of three or more head nods was found to accompany vocalic hesitation, change of subject, or gradual fade away of phonation on the part of the person being interviewed.

Birdwhistell appears to have isolated behaviors which can be used by an interviewer which have an effect on the person being interviewed. This is clearly communicative behavior, though not necessarily linguistic behavior (i.e. the interviewer is not speaking at the time). Though I know of no study of head nodding on the part of speakers, it is obvious that it does occur also.

ASL signers also nod their heads. However, the head nods that I will be discussing in this chapter are those used by the person signing. Their linguistic status cannot be assumed, though their communicative function will be obvious.

I will distinguish several different types of head nods and how each is used. For the head nods discussed in 2.3.1, I will not attempt to establish their linguistic status but will merely describe their communicative value. The main purpose of this will be to distinguish these from the head nod discussed in section 2.3.2, for which I will suggest a linguistic analysis.

2.3.1.1. Rapid slight head nods. In some of the head movements I have examined, a single head nod consists of movement away from a beginning position and a return to that position. In these cases the head does not first move down, return to neutral, move up, return to neutral, move down, etc. Rather, if the initial movement is down, the head will return to the original head position and move down again, etc. This is the case with the rapid slight head nods. These are the fastest type of head nod I have observed in videotapes of ASL utterances. They occur with material which is inserted parenthetically into the ASL sentence structure. The following example should clarify what I mean.

(14)   BILL BROTHER GET JOB
      'Bill, my brother, got a job.'

The line over BROTHER indicates the location of the rapid head nods. Without the rapid head nodding, the string would mean, 'Bill's brother got a job.' Here, however, the signer has inserted the sign BROTHER into the sentence BILL GET JOB to indicate that Bill is the signer's brother. This is functionally equivalent to an appositive (or reduced nonrestrictive relative clause), though I am making no claims about the structure of the ASL example. In addition to the head movement, a specific facial expression is also associated with this parenthetic insertion. This is illustrated in Plate 8.

BROTHER

Plate 8.

This signal is very easy to recognize, and once it is familiar, it can be picked out of conversational signing with no difficulty.

2.3.1.2. Conventional pantomimic head nods. A special head movement indicates 'the making of a decision'. It consists of a single small quick upward movement of the head and a rapid return to the beginning position. Also during this movement the eye gaze is directed away from the addressee and a nonneutral facial activity is present. Although it is associated with making a decision, it does not function like the verb DECIDE. Rather, this nonmanual behavior is associated with what has been called 'role playing'. That is, the speaker adopts someone else's point of view when he does this. For example, consider the following sequence:

		'nod'		
		nonneutral facial activity maintained		
		no eye contact		
(15)	BILL	PRO.3	GO	MOVIE

The signs themselves would mislead someone who was unaware of the significance of the nonmanual activity which has taken place. That is, the signs appear to mean something like, 'Bill, he went to the movie.' This is not even close to the actual message of the utterance. What was actually meant was that Bill decided that some other person (i.e. not himself) went to the movie. It is impossible for there to be coreference between BILL and PRO.3. The reason for this is that by performing the nonmanual signal indicating a decision, maintaining a lack of eye contact and a nonneutral facial expression, the signer adopted the role of Bill, which he keeps as long as he maintains these last two nonmanual behaviors.[4] Thus, Bill in (15) is neither a subject nor an object but a sign which names the role to be adopted. It is followed by 'nod ', which is followed by the clause PRO.3 GO MOVIE. The reason PRO.3 and BILL cannot be coreferential is the same reason that PRO.3 is never coreferential with the speaker. Thus, in order to make reference to Bill, after adopting the role of Bill, the signer must make *first-person reference.*

$$
\begin{array}{ccc}
 & \underline{\text{'nod'}} & \\
 & \underline{\text{nonneutral facial activity maintained}} & \\
 & \underline{\text{no eye contact}} & \\
\text{(16)} \quad \text{BILL} \quad \text{PRO.1} & \text{GO} & \text{MOVIE}
\end{array}
$$

Now the sequence indicates that Bill decided to go to the movie. This particular use of head movement appears to be a special conventional type of pantomimic activity with a conventional meaning attached to it.

There are other pantomimic head nods that I have seen in stories. In the signing of 'The Sorcerer's Apprentice' a signer was explaining that Willabald could make himself disappear and re-appear in a different location. After signing that the magician had reappeared in another location, the signer bowed his head humbly as if he were the magician, then signed that the people applauded.

Another conventional use of head nods occurred in the same story. The signer would pause at times, put his hands together, look slightly up and to the side with his eyes narrowed, and nod his head. This was interpreted as the storyteller's comment to himself that, yes, that was the way it was.

This type of activity appears to be common to both the deaf and the hearing in our culture. The question as to whether or not they have special linguistic status in ASL will be left open here.

2.3.1.3. 'Head dip'. Stokoe (1960) noticed that a tiny nod downward or a slight lowering of the eyes was used in significant ways. On a filmed record of a conversation between two signers, he found that after being asked if he remembered an earlier incident, the addressee responded by saying REMEMBER and simultaneously (or even before the beginning of the sign) there was a 'slight lowering of the eyes, or a tiny nod downward, or both these minute eye and head movements' (1960: 62).

Stokoe found that this type of head movement also occurred in sentences with no explicit subject. For example, one can say ENJOY and simultaneously nod the head, and the subject of ENJOY will be interpreted as the first-person-singular subject. Stokoe took this to mean that the head nod had two functions: to indicate a response, and to indicate a first-person subject (Stokoe 1960: 64).

I have also seen this type of 'head dip' in yes–no questions, but I will not be presenting an analysis of this type of head movement here.

2.3.1.4. Fast head nods. I have observed in my data that if something has been claimed not to be true, a signer can insist on the truth of what he is asserting by employing a rapid series of head nods throughout the utterance. For example, if it had been claimed that the dog didn't chase the cat, a signer could emphasize that the dog *did* chase the cat, in the following way.

<u>rapid   nodding</u>
(17)   DOG CHASE CAT
       'The dog *did* chase the cat.'

Several types of facial expression may accompany this nodding, and it is not clear whether there is a specific facial activity which always occurs with this signal. This head activity may be related to the nonmanual signal 'hn', to be discussed in 2.3.2, but more research will be required in order to make such a claim.

The rate of these nods is approximately two cycles per sign. By cycle, I mean a completed occurrence of a head nod including a return to the neutral head position. The number of cycles is equivalent to the number of downward head movements.

2.3.1.5. Head nods inside clauses. A head nod (or head nods) can occur within clauses. We just saw this in the discussion of the contrastive use of head nods. The first three examples below are from a videotaped narrative, and the fourth was produced in isolation. I have included in the notation the places where the orientation of the face is downward ('d'), upward ('u'), and forward ('f').

(18) $\overline{\text{f}\quad\text{d}\quad\text{f}\quad\text{d f}\quad\text{d}\quad\text{f}}$
      BROOM GET PAIL PICK-UP
      'The broom got the pail and picked it up.'
      [It was a magic broom.]

(19) $\overline{\text{f}\quad\text{d}\qquad\qquad\text{u f}}$
      WILLABALD GO-AWAY
      'Willabald went away.'

(20) $\overline{\qquad\qquad\text{f}\quad\text{d}\quad\text{f}}$
      PRO.3 SENTENCE$_v$. SUCCEED
      'He said the sentence. It worked.'

(21) $\overline{\text{f}\quad\text{d}\quad\text{u}\quad\text{d}\quad\text{f}}$
      PRO.1 LIKE JOHN
      'I like John.'

Recall that the number of cycles corresponds to the number of downward head movements. Thus there are three cycles in (18), one cycle in (19), one cycle in (20), and two cycles in (21). In all these cases, with the exception of SUCCEED, there are fewer nodding cycles than signs. This appears to be the least emphatic form the head nods take. (In the insistence mentioned earlier [2.3.1.4], a sentence like PRO.1 LIKE JOHN could be accompanied by seven nodding cycles. This is more than double the rate shown above.) I have only begun to investigate this clause-internal nodding, but one thing is very clear from the data above: the head–nod cycles are not tied to individual signs. Instead, they must be viewed as a suprasign phenomenon. For example, in the string $\overline{\qquad\text{d}\qquad\qquad\text{u f}}$ WILLABALD GO-AWAY, one cycle is stretched out over the string. In the string $\overline{\qquad\text{d}\quad\text{u}\quad\text{d f}}$ PRO.1 LIKE JOHN, two cycles cover the string. In string $\overline{\text{d}\quad\text{f}\quad\text{d f}\quad\text{d}\quad\text{f}}$ BROOM GET PAIL PICK-UP, one cycle accompanies each of the final two signs, but this is not true of the first two signs.

The syntactic status of these head nods will be left as an open question, though they may be related to the signal 'hn' discussed in the next section.

2.3.2. The head nod 'hn': a possible syntactic analysis

2.3.2.0. Introduction. I have put off the discussion of a larger, slower head movement until now in order to avoid confusion with any of the head movements discussed earlier. That is, it will be helpful to know what kinds of head movements I am not talking about when reading through this section.

The head nod discussed here, 'hn', is larger, deeper, and slower than the head movements discussed earlier. It is much easier to see than the very slight movements mentioned in the previous section. I find 'hn' either within a clause or after a clause. By this I do not mean to imply that all clauses have either an internal nod or a nod following the clause. Many clauses have no nod of any kind that I can see.

If 'hn' follows a clause like DOG CHASE CAT, it is interpreted as emphasizing that what the clause describes really occurred. This appearance of 'hn' appears to be an optional way of emphasizing that the event occurred.

(22)   DOG CHASE CAT
      'The dog chased the cat.'

                      <u>hn</u>
(23)   DOG CHASE CAT
      'The dog did chase the cat.'

The translation I have shown above is the translation given to me by one of the signers I discussed this data with. The two others did not attempt to find a direct English translation, but characterized the head nod 'hn' as emphasizing that the event occurred.

2.3.2.1. Syntactic environments requiring the head nod 'hn'. As we saw above, the string DOG CHASE CAT may or may not be followed by 'hn.' There are syntactic constructions, however, which require the presence of 'hn'. For example, if the verb phrase has been topicalized, the subject must be accompanied by 'hn':

(24) $\overline{\text{t}\overline{\text{hn}}}$[5]
     CHASE CAT DOG
     'As for chasing the cat, the dog did it.'

If only the object had been topicalized, 'hn' would not be required:

(25) $\overline{\text{t}}$
     CAT DOG CHASE
     'As for the cat, the dog chased it.'

Thus we can see that 'hn' is not simply required with a constituent following a topic. Rather it is only required when the subject is left 'stranded'. The fact that the stranded noun must be a subject is illustrated by the following example where the head nod 'hn' is also not required:

(26) $\overline{\text{narrow eyes +q}}$
     JOHN BUY WHAT   DOG[6]
     'What did John buy? — a dog.'

The second construction which requires 'hn' involves the rule of 'gapping' (Ross 1967). An example of gapping in English would be the reduction of the sentences,

(27)   'The boy works in a skyscraper and the girl works in a quonset hut',
by the deletion of the second occurrence of 'works':
(28)   'The boy works in a skyscraper and the girl in a quonset hut.'

(Ross 1967)

ASL can also reduce sentences by gapping. When this occurs, 'hn' accompanies the object of the gapped verb.

(29)   HAVE WONDERFUL PICNIC. PRO.1 BRING SALAD,
       $\overline{\text{hn}}$ $\overline{\text{hn}}$ $\overline{\text{hn}}$
     JOHN BEER, SANDY CHICKEN, TED HAMBURGER.
     'We had a wonderful picnic. I brought the salad, John (brought) the beer, Sandy (brought) the chicken, and Ted (brought) the hamburger.'

In this example the verb BRING occurs only once. It has apparently been deleted from each of the following clauses by the rule of gapping.[7]

In the two environments mentioned above, 'hn' always occurs in my data. In the following two environments 'hn' always occurs given certain circumstances.

To say that John is a doctor requires only two signs in ASL: JOHN and DOCTOR. What has not been noticed about this type of sentence is that 'hn' appears simultaneously with the sign DOCTOR (provided that JOHN DOCTOR is a main clause). Without the head nod 'hn', the string would be interpreted as 'John's doctor'. This appears to be parallel to the previous two examples where 'hn' was required: a surface main clause with a subject but no verb.

It may not be immediately obvious that DOCTOR is a noun in surface structure. The sign DOCTOR, however, will not undergo any of the inflections which verbs in ASL can undergo. It can also not be modified by the adverbial nonmanual signals discussed later in this chapter (cf. 2.4).

There is one more syntactic environment where 'hn' appears, given certain circumstances. Often a signer will repeat a pronoun coreferential with the subject of a sentence immediately after the sentence. If the sentence contains no internal head nod, then 'hn' obligatorily accompanies the repeated pronoun:[8]

<u>   hn   </u>

(30)   MAN BUY CAR PRO.3
       'The man bought a car, he did.'

<u>   hn   </u>

(31)   MAN SATISFIED PRO.3
       'The man is satisfied, he is.'

There is one special property of 'hn' which should be mentioned: 'hn' is closely tied to assertion. That is, in each of the examples discussed above where 'hn' appears, the speaker is making an assertion. It appears that if the signer is not asserting a given clause, 'hn' does not felicitously appear with that clause.

<u>   hn   </u>

(32)   ?? PRO.1 DOUBT JOHN DOCTOR
       'I doubt that John is a doctor.'

The signers I have consulted feel that (32) is contradictory; this is apparently because they are asserting that they doubt that John is a doctor and simultaneously, because of the presence of 'hn', asserting that John is a doctor.

2.3.2.2. A possible analysis.

How are we to account for the presence of 'hn'? Someone might argue that this is a type of intonation and that certain sentence types require a certain type of intonation. This does not solve any problems about how 'hn' functions, what it means, and where it is required to occur — it merely gives another name to the nonmanual behavior we are attempting to understand.

Consistent with all the data I have been able to gather would be an analysis with 'hn' as an affirmative or assertive morpheme within a nonsubordinate clause (perhaps as a daughter of S).

(33)

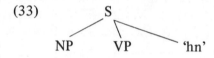

When 'hn' does not have a lexical verb as a clausemate, its presence would be obligatory (with the exceptions noted earlier).

2.3.2.3. A possible parallel with the English auxiliary verbs 'be' and 'do'.

The fact that when 'hn' is required no lexical verb is present, taken together with the way the presence of 'hn' is translated, suggests that a reasonable way of approaching 'hn' in these structures is to analyze it in a way similar to the way that Langacker and Munro (1975) analyze the auxiliary verbs 'be' and 'do' in English.[9]

Langacker has claimed that the verbs 'be' and 'do' are predicates of existence in English. He has further claimed that the semantic structure of any sentence in English will contain one or the other of these predicates. 'Be' predicates the existence of a state, and 'do' predicates the existence of a process.

Thus, all sentences in English which characterize a process rather than a state have the existential predicate DO_p in their semantic representations such that the clause structure which is subordinate to it structurally is within its scope. Thus, the English sentence 'Martin lives' would have the following as part of its semantic representation.

(34)

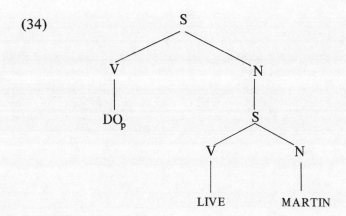

Langacker points out that the predicate DO is not necessarily realized on the surface. That is, the structure above is part of the semantic representation of the sentence 'Martin lives' even though DO_p is not realized on the surface. Under certain circumstances, however, the predicate DO_p is realized on the surface:

(35) emphasis: Martin *does* (still) live.
     negation: Martin does not (still) live.
     questions: Does Martin (still) live?
     ellipsis: Martin (still) lives, and so does Jill.
                    (Langacker and Munro 1975: 357)

Instead of a rule of 'do-support,' as in Chomsky (1965), which inserts 'do' where it does occur, Langacker proposes that there is a rule of 'do deletion' which deletes 'do' in those cases where it does not appear.[10]

Does it make any sense to talk about a suprasegmental existential predicate in ASL? The ASL examples presented earlier suggest that it might.

2.3.2.4. 'hn' as an existential predicate. Here I would like to examine the consequences of supposing that 'hn' is an existential predicate which predicates the existence of a state or process, and that when it is realized on the surface, it has the form of the head nod 'hn'.

The semantic representation of DOG CHASE CAT would contain, in part, the following schematic structure:

(36)

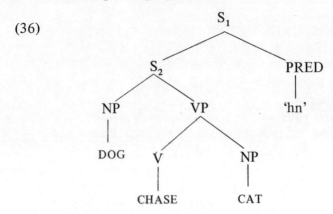

The predicate 'hn' need not show up on the surface. However, for emphasis it will show up.

(37)   DOG CHASE CAT
'The dog chased the cat.'

<pre>
                    hn
</pre>
(38)   DOG CHASE CAT
'The dog did chase the cat.'

The head nod following the clause DOG CHASE CAT appears to be emphasizing that the event took place (exists). This is exactly what would be expected given the semantic structure illustrated above.

According to Langacker and Munro (1975) this is exactly the function carried out by the auxiliary 'do' in English. He claims that it predicates the existence of a process. This can be seen in the following way.

A speaker of English knows that there is more than one way to say, 'The dog did chase the cat.' The way that I am interested in here carries no contrastive stress on 'did'. This type of reading of the sentence sounds funny in isolation, but the following context may help: Two people are told that a dog will chase a cat and are instructed to go into a certain room after that happens. They look out the window and see a cat and a dog lying down. Suddenly the dog starts chasing the cat. The two individuals look at each other, and one says, 'Well, the dog did chase the cat, just as they said it would. We better go in.' Notice that there is no argumentation here about whether or not the event took place. The presence of 'do' in this case, according to Langacker's analysis, is an explicit indicator that the event took place. This is exactly how the signers characterized the head nod 'hn' when explaining it to me.[11]

We will now turn to the constructions in which the presence of the head nod 'hn' is required. The first is illustrated below:

                        t   hn
(39)   CHASE CAT DOG.
       'As for chasing the cat, the dog did it.'

In this sentence the verb phrase has been topicalized, and as a result is no longer part of the main clause. In fact, the main clause only contains one sign − DOG. The hypothetical structure of this string is shown below:

(40)

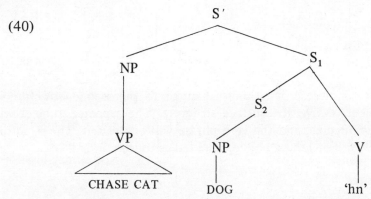

In this configuration the only verb in the main clause is the existential predicate 'hn', and it shows up in surface structure. That is, the signer nods his head while signing DOG.[12]

In addition, when these sentence types are translated, signers emphasize that it means that the dog *did* it (chase the cat). Once again this is to be expected given the schematic semantic representation in which the head nod is a meaningful predicate in semantic structure.

Recall that if a pronoun *coreferential with the subject* of a sentence is repeated at the end of the sentence, it is accompanied by 'hn'.

                    hn
(41)   BILL BUY CAR PRO.3
       'Bill bought a car, he did.'

This is one more structure in which there is a 'stranded' noun with
no lexical verb associated with it. In this case the stranded noun
is coreferential with the *subject* of the sentence it follows. The
structure suggests that there is a very intimate connection between
the first clause and the repeated pronoun. This suggests an analysis
in which the source of (41) consists of two identical clauses (at
some level) and an eventual reduction of the repeated clause
through ellipsis.

(42)

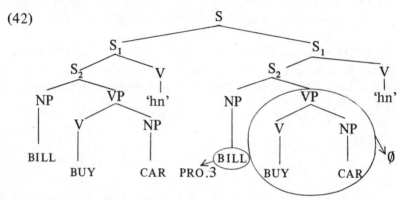

I have indicated what must happen to the second structure in
order to derive the surface structure. The repeated subject will
pronominalize, and the verb phrase will be deleted. The structure
which will be left can be represented as follows:

(43)

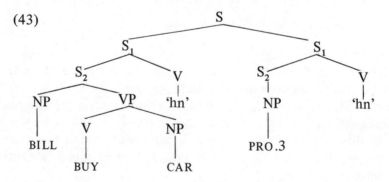

Each structure contains 'hn'. In the second structure 'hn' sur-
faces (presumably) because there is no lexical verb. For even
more emphasis, 'hn' can also surface in the first structure.[13]

In the above examples the head nod 'hn' has cooccurred with
an action (DOG CHASE CAT), and a process (BILL BUY CAR)

which is not an action. In the next example the head nod 'hn' is present in a sentence which expresses a stative relationship. Recall that to say that John is a doctor requires only two signs in ASL: JOHN and DOCTOR (in that order), and a head nod accompanying the sign DOCTOR.

(44)   <u>   hn   </u>
         JOHN DOCTOR
         'John is a doctor.'

Without the head nod the sequence would be interpreted as the phrase, 'John's doctor'. Apparently the head nod shows up here because there is no other verb. This is consistent with the previous cases where either an isolated pronoun (subject) or the subject itself was 'stranded' with no lexical verb.

The final syntactic constructions which require the presence of 'hn' are those in which gapping has applied.

(45)   <u>   hn   </u>   <u>   hn </u>
      PRO.1 BRING SALAD, JOHN BEER, SANDY CHICKEN,
                    <u> hn </u>
      TED HAMBURGER.

'I brought the salad, John (brought) the beer, Sandy (brought) the chicken, and Ted (brought) the hamburger.'

In (45) the verb in the second, third, and fourth clauses has been gapped, leaving behind the subject and the object. We can represent the structures of these clauses in the following way.

(46)

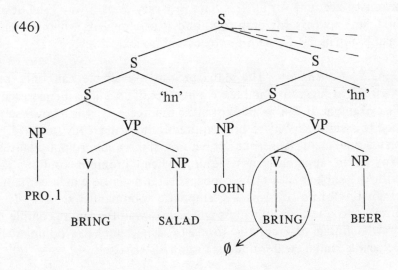

Once again, in each of the surface clauses containing a subject without a lexical verb, 'hn' obligatorily shows up.[14]

Notice that in each of the well-formed cases, where the main clause contained no lexical verb, the head nod 'hn' was coterminous with the final noun in the clause rather than coming after the clause. According to the analysis being considered here, this would remedy the lack of a verb *in* the clause because 'hn' would be within the clause.

Has the postulation of predicate status for the head nod 'hn' been helpful in accounting for the occurrence of the head nod?

A signer sometimes nods his head after a sentence. When he does, it appears to emphasize that what the signer had just signed was in fact true. We also saw that sometimes this head nod is accompanied by a pronoun coreferential with the subject of the sentence. This emphasizes that what was predicated of the subject was in fact true.

A head nod also occurs when the verb and object have been topicalized, leaving the subject 'stranded' with no lexical verb. In this instance the interpretation is that the subject *did* something.

Also, in a main clause which normally contains no lexical verb (JOHN DOCTOR) the head nod 'hn' also appears. Finally, in a clause where the verb has been gapped, leaving a derived structure with no lexical verb, 'hn' appears obligatorily.

The postulation of a nonlexical predicate of existence, which when realized on the surface appears in the form of a head nod, seems to account for all this data in a very elegant way. The head nod 'hn' appears for emphasis, and it also appears when it commands a main clause with a subject and no lexical verb.

2.3.2.5. Conclusion. The data presently available can only be regarded as suggestive and leave a number of questions unanswered. For example, if 'hn' is an existential predicate, why is it so closely tied to assertion? Why is 'hn' required if the string JOHN DOCTOR is an asserted main clause, but not required if it is a subordinate clause? Why is 'hn' apparently not required when a pronoun coreferential with the subject of a clause appears after a clause which contains emphatic forms of signs or 'emphatic' nonmanual signals? The answers to questions like these will have to wait for a more complete understanding of emphatic forms of signs, emphatic nonmanual behaviors, and a clearer understanding of 'hn' itself.

2.3.3. Side to side headshakes

Some side-to-side headshakes have a negating function. I emphasize *some*, because whether or not a headshake can negate depends
on the accompanying facial expression and also on the vertical
orientation of the head. Plate 9 illustrates a facial expression and

		n
DOG	CHASE	CAT

Plate 9.

head orientation which can accompany the side-to-side negating
headshake. The head movement itself appears to be no different
from that which would stand as the answer to a yes–no question.
I will symbolize the combination of the side-to-side headshake and
the facial expression shown in Plate 9 as 'n'.

There are two parts to this facial expression accompanying the
headshake: the eyes and the lower face. The eyes are narrowed.
The position of the lips appears to be affected by three different
muscle groups. One group is pulling the sides of the mouth down,
another is pushing up the lower lip, and a third is raising the
upper lip.[15]

The negative headshake, like the head nod discussed in 2.3.1.5,
also occurs either during a clause or after it.[16] It differs from the
previously analyzed head nod in that, if it follows the clause, the
clause is specially marked. That is, you may not sign a sentence
with a neutral facial expression and follow that with the negative
headshake. Instead, the clause is marked with a signal such as
'narrow eyes + q' (47) or the signal 't'. Example (47) is taken
from a signed version of 'The Sorcerer's Apprentice'.

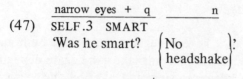

(47)   SELF.3   SMART
      'Was he smart? {No / headshake}?'

(48)   JOHN GET MONEY
      'As for John's getting any money, he didn't.'

Alternatively, the negative headshake cooccurs with all the signs in the sentence being negated. All the signs which cooccur with the headshake fall under the scope of the negation.

$$\overline{\qquad\qquad\qquad\text{n}}$$

(49)   WOMAN FORGET PURSE
      'It is not the case that the woman forgot the purse.'

These two examples illustrate the two ways that I have seen the negative headshake used with a sign string that contains no manual negation. A proper analysis of this headshake would require a full analysis of lexical negation, since the two do interact. That is, negative lexical items such as NOT, NOT-YET, NEVER, etc., are often accompanied by a side-to-side headshake. To the best of my knowledge, the interaction between these has never been seriously studied. One possible analysis of the negative headshake would be that it represents the surface realization of an underlying single predicate of negation; distinct from the lexical sign NOT. In this analysis the underlying structure of WOMAN FORGET PURSE could be represented, in part, by the simplified structure below:

(50)

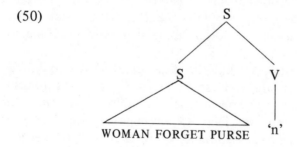

On the other hand the negative headshake could be analyzed as being equivalent to the English speaker saying 'no' (or shaking his head 'no') as in the English translation of (47). In this analysis the negating headshake would not be analyzed as a higher verb of negation, but as a way of denying a previously mentioned possibility as in (47), or as a way of denying something as it is being said as in (49).

The headshake 'n' and the head nod 'hn' do not cooccur. The reason for this may be physiological or it may be semantic. It would be very difficult (or at least dizzying) to shake the head sideways and simultaneously nod the head up and down. On the other hand, if the negative headshake means 'no', it would be very strange indeed to assert the existence of something and simultaneously to say 'no' to that assertion. As a result of this confusing evidence, the syntactic status of the negative headshake will be left open.

The question of how much reduction (or variation) in the facial expression and headshake can take place while still signalling negation will also be left open. Bellugi and Fischer (1972) and Baker (1976a) report that a frown and lowered eyebrows are sufficient for signalling negation; however, I have been unable to confirm that finding.

I believe that what these investigators have described is probably a signal which expresses doubt, or something similar, on the part of the signer. I have never seen, nor has a signer, through introspection, been able to give me an example of, a facial expression which alone will negate a sentence.

Such an expression of doubt would be appropriate if the signer was unsure of the truth value of the sentence he was uttering, but would not negate the sentence. For example, if a signer used such an expression with the sign sequence WOMAN FORGET PURSE it might indicate that the signer was unsure about whether or not the woman forgot the purse. A signer could accurately say that the sentence would be appropriate if the woman had not forgotten the purse, but this would not indicate that the sentence means, 'The woman didn't forget the purse.'

2.4. NONMANUAL ADVERBS

2.4.1. 'mm'

Some ASL sentences seem to convey much more information than would be expected given the translations of the individual signs in the sentence. For example, the sentence transcribed as

MAN FISH[I: continuous] was translated by several native signers as

'The man was fishing with relaxation and enjoyment.'[17] While it is true that in sentence formation, because of the nature of syntax, the whole is greater than the sum of its parts, it seemed a little strange that the meaning 'with relaxation and enjoyment' would be a natural result of syntactic structure alone (i.e. syntactic structure provides information about the relationships between the arguments and the verb or topicalization but is not known to provide information like 'relaxation' or 'enjoyment'). As a matter of fact a special nonmanual signal, illustrated below, accompanied the

verb FISH[I: continuous]. This nonmanual signal seemed a possible

carrier of this extra information. On examining other sentences with the unaccounted-for information, 'with relaxation and enjoyment', I found the same facial expression and head position were present during the verb sign. This nonmanual signal, 'mm', is shown in Plate 10.

mm
_____
FISH[I: continuous]

Plate 10.

The significant part of the nonmanual signal which accompanies FISH [I: continuous] is the configuration of the lips. It is accomplished by keeping the lips together and pushing them out without puckering (hence the notation 'mm'). The head position shown, with the head back and turned to one side, is the position I generally see, but under special circumstances others occur.

If this nonmanual signal were not present in the string MAN FISH [I:continuous], the translation would be the expected 'The man is fishing.' The same is true of all the other examples of sentences containing this particular nonmanual signal which I have recorded. Thus, a very general process superimposes a nonmanual signal on a verb with adverbial effect. Even though it is not a manual sign, it has the effect of a manually produced sign.

A word in spoken language or a sign in ASL which carried the information carried by 'mm' would automatically be assumed to be functioning as part of the linguistic structure of the language. In fact, this seems like a very reasonable assumption to make. However, here, where we are dealing with nonmanual signals, we will also try to demonstrate that 'mm', and signals like it, are part of the linguistic structure of the utterance.

An attempt will be made to see if the 'mm' signal will fall within the scope of questioning or negation. Failure to do so will tell us nothing about the linguistic status of 'mm', since many things which are clearly linguistic cannot be questioned (i.e. in the yes–no question, 'Is it red or green?', *or* is not being questioned). On the other hand, if the 'mm' signal is part of a yes–no question, or subject to negation, it will be assumed that the 'mm' signal is indeed part of the linguistic structure of the utterance.

If the same sequence of signs and the 'mm' signal are signed as a yes–no question, we find that the nonmanual grammatical signal, 'q', (i.e. brows up, head and body forward) which covers the entire sentence, is superimposed on the nonmanual adverbial signal, 'mm', which covers the verb. This question is illustrated in Plate 11.

Notice that the eyebrows are raised and the head and body are leaned forward throughout the sentence. Also notice the special 'mm' mouth configuration during the verb. Apparently, the head position (tilted to the side) which we saw in the statement (Plate

	q
	mm
MAN	FISH [I:continuous]

Plate 11.

10) need not occur in the question. It is easy to see that during the verb sign FISH [I:continuous], the two separate nonmanual signals are present.[18]

The point of this example syntactically is that the nonmanual adverb, 'mm', falls within the scope of the question. The question asked is, 'Is the man fishing with relaxed enjoyment?' and not simply, 'Is the man fishing?' Since the 'relaxed enjoyment' is part of the question, if the man is fishing in any other way the answer to the question is 'no'. Of course, the answer is also 'no' if the man is relaxing but not fishing, etc.

The 'mm' expression also falls within the scope of negation. This can be seen in the sentence,

> ```
>                         mm
> ```
> (51)   MAN NOT FISH [I:continuous]
>   'The man is not fishing with relaxed enjoyment.'

The above sentence is true if the man is not fishing or if the man is not relaxing. That is, the man could be fishing intensely or simply relaxing near the water. The point again is that the nonmanual signal is part of the syntactic structure of the sentence (if such phenomena as falling within the scope of questioning or negation are diagnostic of syntactic structure).

This suggests analyzing 'mm' as an adverb, even though it is not a manually produced sign. The following is not an unreasonable first approximation of the sentence in Plate 11,

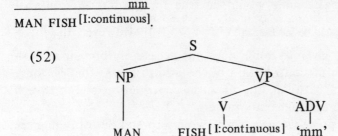

MAN FISH [I:continuous].

(52)

The 'mm' under the adverb node in the tree above represents the nonmanual signal responsible for the interpretation of 'relaxation and enjoyment'.

This nonmanual adverb is not always interpreted as carrying the meaning, 'with relaxation and enjoyment'. It can also be interpreted as meaning that everything is 'normal and proper' in the situation being described. For example, 'mm' can be used with the verb sign I will gloss as ENGINE-RUNNING. The sign is made as illustrated in Plate 12 (with the fingers wiggling). If it is accompanied by the 'mm' adverb, the sentence is interpreted to mean that the engine is working properly — nothing is wrong.

<u>_____mm</u>
ENGINE-RUNNING

Plate 12.

The sentence MAN <u>FIGURE-OUT</u> has two English interpretations (provided by native signers): 'The man is figuring something out with enjoyment', and 'The man is just plain figuring something out' (i.e. there is nothing wrong or out of the ordinary about what he is doing). The same would be true for the interpretation of sentences like MAN $\overline{\text{WALK}}^{\text{mm}}$, or PRO.1 $\overline{\text{WATCH}}^{\text{mm}}$. However, the interpretation of a given example does not necessarily provide us with the true semantic contribution of the adverb itself. That is, there is a difference between the semantic contribution of the adverb and the way the string is interpreted.

Up to this point we have seen two interpretations of sequences containing the nonmanual signal, 'mm'. No claims have been made about the exact semantic contribution of the 'mm' signal when considered in isolation. One possibility is that 'mm' could have two separate meanings which it could contribute to the verb it accompanies: one connected with 'relaxation and enjoyment' and one where things are 'normal and proper'. The problem with this possibility is that if 'mm' accompanies a verb like ENGINE-RUNNING, there should be two readings: 'relaxed enjoyment' and 'normal and proper'. In fact, there is only the 'normal and proper' reading. Similarly, if 'mm' accompanies a verb like WALK, the combination is not felt by native signers to be ambiguous. The two readings apparently come about as a result of trying to find a term to describe the meaning of the combination. That is, 'mm' should be considered as a predicate with a single semantic contribution. Unfortunately, it is difficult to pin down exactly what that contribution is.

The following approximate the basic meaning of 'mm': 'nothing special', 'ordinary', 'unimpeded', and 'normal and proper'. 'Nothing special' and 'ordinary' are both insufficient in that if things are ordinarily bad or improper then 'mm' would not be used. 'Unimpeded' also has the same problem. Things can be unimpeded and improper, etc. 'Normal and proper' seems to fit both the ENGINE-RUNNING case where the engine is running normally and properly and the cases like WALK where normal and proper walking is unhurried, relaxed, etc.

In this section we saw examples of a nonmanual signal which we analyzed as an adverb. This signal has a broad application to a large class of lexical items in ASL. It was found to be coterminous with the verbs in the examples presented here. We shall see examples later where nonmanual adverbs are coterminous with and used to add a specific meaning to lexical adverbs as well. The semantic contributions of the verb and the nonmanual adverb are separable. The nonmanual adverb 'mm' has a specific meaning which it adds to the verbs it accompanies. This was analyzed as centering around 'normal and proper', 'ordinary', and 'unimpeded'. The nonmanual adverb was found to fall within the scope of questioning and negation. This was taken as evidence that the signal was indeed part of the syntactic structure of the utterance.

I would not want to make the claim that every occurrence of this nonmanual behavior is necessarily adverbial. For example, the discussion has been limited to a definable class of signs (i.e. verbs) and a specific temporal relationship between the manual sign and the nonmanual signal (i.e. they are coterminous). It may not even be the case that given these conditions the nonmanual signal is an adverb. For example, in 2.1 we saw that a sign made like SUNRISE but with an F handshape, accompanied by a specific facial expression, was interpreted as 'sleep-in'. The particular facial expression was 'mm'. 'mm' may be functioning as an adverb here, but it could also be the case that the manual sign and the nonmanual signal have formed a lexical unit and are regarded as a single sign rather than a combination of a manual sign and an adverb.[19]

2.4.2. 'cs'

There is a specific facial expression and body posture which is part of a modulation of certain time adverbs in ASL. In its citation form, RECENTLY, for example, is signed with the facial expression shown in Plate 13a; when recency is being contrasted with a much greater period of time (e.g. not last week – just recently), the signer's head leans and turns toward the side of the body on which RECENTLY is being made, and the shoulder on that side (or both sides) is pulled forward and raised; the facial expression is also made more intense by a greater contraction of the same facial muscles (see Plate 13b). Among other things all this activity brings the cheek and shoulder closer together (hence the notation 'cs'). Variation in the intensity of these movements is possible depending on how much contrast the signer wants to provide.

Other past-tense adverbials like PAST TUESDAY, YESTERDAY

a. RECENTLY   b. RECENTLY

Plate 13.

NIGHT, and LAST-YEAR (see Plate 14) undergo the same modulations. NOW undergoes a similar modulation as do such future adverbials as NEXT-YEAR, NEXT-WEEK, and TOMORROW MORNING.

a. LAST-YEAR   b. LAST-YEAR

Plate 14.

When such adverbial phrases consist of two signs (e.g. YESTERDAY NIGHT) they are signed as a compound and both signs are accompanied by the nonmanual signal. If the adverbial sign has a path of movement rather than a local movement, the length of the path of movement is reduced and is made closer to the shoulder.[20]

This nonmanual signal also occurs with verbs. Consider the following sequence:

                  —————— cs
(53)   TRAIN ARRIVE
        'The train is about to arrive.'
        'The train just arrived.'

The notation 'cs' represents the nonmanual signal under discussion. As can be seen from the translations, the nonmanual signal, 'cs', is not simply a substitution for the manual sign RECENTLY, since RECENTLY is a past-tense adverbial and 'cs' is not specified for tense.

The same nonmanual adverb occurs when a signer wishes to stress close *physical* proximity. In signing that someone was standing *right* next to something, the signer would employ this expression. This particular nonmanual signal, in each instance, communicates close proximity. With the time adverbials the added expression indicates — with LAST-YEAR, for example — that it was not long ago, but near to the present. In the last example, the close proximity is physical rather than temporal.

The fact that the 'cs' signal can occur with verbs as well as adverbs is significant. The 'cs' signal is not simply an idiosyncratic property of adverbial phrases. If it were, it would be less interesting. However, 'cs' can cooccur with verbs as well as adverbs and in such a way that there is always one common semantic contribution — proximity (temporal or spatial).

As the following example shows, this adverbial signal can also fall under the scope of questioning.

                             q
   —————————————————————————
                             cs
(54)   HAPPEN YESTERDAY NIGHT
        'Did it happen just last night?'

This nonmanual signal can also be naturally analyzed as adverbial. Consider the form meaning 'just last night'. The following figure illustrates how this adverbial phrase could be analyzed:

(55)

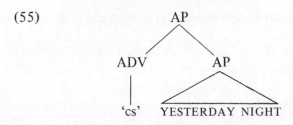

In the case of the person standing right next to something, the nonmanual signal, 'cs', would be modifying the predicate which indicated where the person was standing.

2.4.3. 'th'

'th' is a nonmanual adverb whose semantic contribution centers around lack of control, inattention, unintention, and unawareness. The head is tilted and the tongue is protruded through the lips (hence the notation 'th'). To produce the correct lip configuration, the lips must be pushed out. The upper lip is also slightly curled upward.[21] This nonmanual signal was present in the sentence MAN DRIVE[I: continuous], in a story created by the signer in Plate 15.

th

MAN   DRIVE[I:continuous]

Plate 15.

In the story the man thought he was really driving a car on a road, but in reality the car was not moving. It was in a movie studio, and the man wasn't driving at all. The nonmanual signal, 'th', in this case, indicates the man's unawareness. Once again, the nonmanual signal is clearly performing an adverbial function. Of course, in another context the signer could use a different nonmanual signal with exactly the same signs. For example, he could use the 'mm' adverb during the verb sign DRIVE[I:continuous] to indicate that the man was driving with relaxation and enjoyment.

On one of the videotapes this nonmanual signal occurs with the sign FALL-ASLEEP. This occurred in a story where the character in the story had been abducted and, after some frantic activity, fell asleep. The meaning here, with this combination of the nonmanual signal 'th' and the sign FALL-ASLEEP, is that the character in the story fell asleep not through any intent on her part but through lack of control (i.e. it was unintended).

If a 1-classifier (an erect index finger representing a person) moves smoothly and quickly something like this

while being accompanied by the 'th' signal, the consistent interpretation of this combination of manual and nonmanual signals is that the person represented by the classifier went by without regard to the signer; or that he passed between the signer and the person the signer was talking to — interrupting their conversation.[22]

Plate 16 shows the same nonmanual signal used with sign STAND. In this case the nonmanual signal indicates a lack of awareness.

'th' can also be used with the previously illustrated sign ENGINE-RUNNING. I have discussed this with several signers and all agreed that it means that the car was left running unattended while the driver was gone.[23]

To ask if a car had been left running with no driver around, the signer would simply superimpose the nonmanual yes–no question signal 'q' on the sentence CAR ENGINE-RUNNING.

<u>   th   </u>
STAND

Plate 16.

<u>   q   </u>
<u>   th </u>
(56)   CAR ENGINE-RUNNING

In the proper context, the nonmanual adverb can convey inattention as it does in the following example.

               <u>   th   </u>
(57)   PRO.1 GO-ACROSS. WRONG,ACCIDENT
       'I crossed the street carelessly. Whoops! There was an
       accident.'

In the following example, the nonmanual signal indicates
getting off the point of the discussion, unintentionally.

                   <u>   th   </u>
(58)   PRO.1 OFF-THE-POINT, TALK, NOW ON-THE-POINT
       'I strayed off the point, talked, and now I'm back on the
       point (of the discussion).'

In 2.4.1 we mentioned that a sign made like SUNRISE but with
an F handshape and the nonmanual signal 'mm' may have formed
a lexical unit meaning 'sleep-in'. The same handshape, movement,
and orientation of the hands, if accompanied by 'th', may also
have formed a lexical unit meaning 'oversleep'. 'th' also occurs
with certain signs when they are made in list form (i.e. OVER-
LOOK). These may be cases of lexical units rather than verb–
adverb combinations.

2.4.4. Summary

We have examined three nonmanual signals and analyzed them as adverbs which form part of the syntactic structure of ASL sentences. These adverbs have broad application to a large class of lexical items in ASL. They are coterminous with the lexical items that they modify, and each of the three adverbs examined was found to add a specific semantic contribution to the lexical item(s) that it was coterminous with. The kind of evidence considered as to whether or not these signals were part of the syntactic structure of the ASL sentences examined consisted of whether or not the semantic contribution of the adverb was subject to questioning or negation. Failure to fall under the scope of questioning and negation would tell us nothing about the syntactic status of these signals, but the fact that they were subject to questioning and negation was taken as evidence that they were indeed part of the syntactic structure.

2.5. SIGNALS FOR EMOTIONAL STATES

2.5.1. The grammatical status of 'surprise'

Certainly signers, like everyone else, use facial expressions which communicate emotions like surprise, fear, or anger. Such expressions often accompany the signs for these emotions. At times, however, the nonmanual signal is superimposed on a sign sequence which makes no mention of emotional states. Plate 17 illustrates,

| PRO.1 | LIKE | JOHN |

Plate 17.

for instance, how a signer conveyed the English sentence, 'I was surprised that I like John', by signing PRO.1 LIKE JOHN, together with the nonmanual signals illustrated. The dropped jaw and the wide eyes used by the signer are claimed to be universal features of surprise (Ekman and Friesen 1975). What cannot be easily seen in the illustration is the nonconstancy of the facial behavior, the head position, and the body movement. In contrast to the non-manual grammatical markers and nonmanual adverbs, these signals do not appear, remain relatively constant, and then disappear. Rather, the expression 'develops' and changes during the string, the body moves forward (generally), and the head does not stay fixed. Typically the head moves down, forward, and 'up. The result is a sequence in which the signer appears to be coming to the realization that she likes John. The point of this discussion is that this is not a 'fixed' signal like the others we have seen previously; it can change throughout the sequence rather than remaining relatively fixed.

It is important to distinguish between being surprised, using a facial expression to convey surprise, and using a facial expression as part of a linguistic system to denote the state of surprise. While Ekman and Friesen point out that the expression of surprise is briefly conveyed by 'fleeting facial expression' (1975: 6) – in the ASL sentence, the signer spreads the surprise behavior over the sequence; it can even continue a short time after the manual signing has stopped. The expression above is not the physiological expression of the emotion but an emblem for conveying meaning. We will look at possible diagnostics to determine the linguistic status of such emblems.

In Plate 17 the subject of the sentence and the speaker are the same, and it is not clear whether the nonmanual behavior is the speaker's way of communicating surprise or whether it is a reflection of surprise to be associated with the subject of the verb. If the sentence were BILL LIKE JOHN instead of PRO.1 LIKE JOHN, would the nonmanual signals illustrated indicate that Bill was surprised that he likes John or that I was surprised that Bill likes John? Signers tell me that the latter is the correct interpretation. This demonstrates that the nonmanual expression of surprise, in the absence of manual signs for surprise, indicates speaker surprise (which may or may not be genuine), not surprise on the part of the subject of the sentence.

Another indication that the signal may not be part of the sentence structure is that it does not fall within the scope of questioning or negation. For example, consider the string BILL LIKE JOHN with nonmanual surprise signals beginning with the sign BILL and signed as a yes–no question with the nonmanual grammatical signal 'q' superimposed throughout the sentence, shown in Plate 18. This question does not ask if I am surprised that Bill likes John. Rather, what it conveys is speaker surprise that Bill likes John, while asking for confirmation. This sentence would occur as a

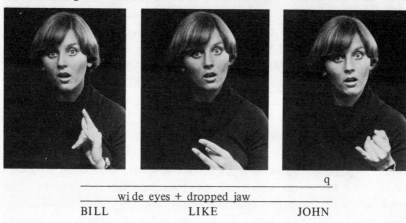

$$\overline{\underline{\text{wide eyes + dropped jaw}}}^{\text{q}}$$

BILL   LIKE   JOHN

Plate 18.

a repetition of something which was just said or learned, showing surprise and asking for confirmation. The point is that the surprise is not being questioned. Similarly, the nonmanual surprise signal isn't negatable. Thus the 'surprise' signals discussed here, unlike the nonmanual adverbs discussed in the previous section, provide no evidence that they are part of the surface clausal structure of the clause they accompany. If they were to find their way into a semantic tree structure, the evidence suggests that the proper place would be at the performative level (i.e. I am asking you with surprise $[\overline{\text{BILL LIKE JOHN}}^{\text{q}}]_S$, etc.).

2.5.2. 'Surprise' in role playing

The same three signs in the same order but with a change in the timing and the nonmanual signals *can* result in the meaning, 'Bill was surprised that he likes John.' This can occur when a signer is adopting a role (cf. section 2.3.1.2). Adopting a role is common in stories and everyday conversation. It can be used for direct quotation or for pantomimic reenactment of an event. The former function is illustrated by JOHN YES. The first sign identifies the person whose role is being adopted. What follows is the direct quotation. The sequence JOHN YES, with the appropriate non-manual behaviors, means 'John said, "yes".' I have even seen role playing done with an animal to indicate what the animal was thinking. In a situation where a dog had a desire to get into a house and circumstances changed so that the dog could get in, a signer signed DOG, looked from side to side as if checking to see if the coast was clear, then signed FINE, meaning the dog thought, 'fine!', now it would have a chance to get in. (Signed with other nonmanual behaviors the sequence could mean, 'The dog is fine.')

In order to determine what nonmanual behaviors were involved, photographs of ASL sequences which signers said included role playing were placed next to one another for comparison. In sequences where an isolated noun preceded the role playing, the photos which accompanied those nouns were all extremely similar. The face itself was very nearly neutral with the head slightly tilted back and to the side, and with no 'eye contact' with the addressee (camera). In each case the interpretation was that the noun was not part of the role-playing sequence, but named the role being adopted. Immediately after this, some pantomimic activity was present and *preceded* any further signing. For example, in the DOG FINE sequence, the sign DOG was made with the 'neutral' expression and head position discussed above. After the sign DOG and before the sign FINE, the signer looked around, moving the head from side to side as if he were really looking to see if the coast was clear. Then when FINE was signed, it was interpreted as the dog's 'comment' on the situation. Bendixen (1975) mentions similar aspects of role playing and also points out the importance of the speaker's lack of eye contact with the addressee during the initial pantomimic 'role establishment' and the subsequent role playing.[24] The sequence BILL LIKE JOHN, with the appropriate facial expression and head position during the sign BILL and subsequent pantomimic activity *before*

LIKE, would be interpreted as a role-playing sequence. This is illustrated in Plate 19.

The fact that Bill says LIKE JOHN instead of PRO.1 LIKE JOHN is not significant. It is quite common for the signer to omit the sign PRO.1 in such simple sentences. Here the unspecified subject of LIKE is assumed to be the signer. Since the signer has adopted the role of Bill, Bill is the one who was surprised. Also notice that BILL is no longer the subject of the verb LIKE. The subject of the verb LIKE is an unspecified first-person singular subject. BILL simply names the identity of the role being played. Thus, without paying attention to the nonmanual signals *it is not even possible to know whether a given sign is the subject of a verb.*

BILL   LIKE   JOHN

Plate 19.

2.5.3. *'Anger'*

Another collection of nonmanual signals which function like the surprise signals are those which indicate anger. Two signers, on separate occasions, were asked to produce the string FEEL-LIKE[+] JOHN GO-OUT SUNBATHE ('I wish the hell John would go out and sunbathe') on videotape. The sign FEEL-LIKE[+] is the emphatic form which I have very roughly translated 'wish the hell'. The two signers produced remarkably similar expressions. Both signers dropped their jaw, bared their teeth, drew their eyebrows down and together, and tensed their lower eyelids. They both used facial expressions of anger. Their expression did not stay fixed or frozen throughout the sequence of signs. Both signers varied both their eyes and their mouths: the man narrowed his eyes till they were almost closed, and the woman actually tightly closed her eyes during two signs. While her eyes were closed, the woman also had her lips tensed and closed.

Both signers showed anger in three areas of the face: the brows, the eyes, and the lower face. This is in agreement with the finding of Ekman and Friesen (1975: 88), who claim that across cultures the facial signals for anger are different from the facial signals for either surprise or fear in requiring involvement of all three areas of the face for an unambiguous signal (the brows, the eyes, and the lower face).

This nonmanual expression of anger is like the nonmanual surprise signal — a state to be associated with the speaker.

Notice that the *functions* we are discussing here — the expressions of a state to be associated with the speaker — are certainly not unique to ASL nor are the forms that they assume. Tone of voice and intonation also perform this function in spoken language (and so does facial activity). English has ways of varying the intonation and voice quality which can indicate surprise or anger on the part of the speaker. In fact, the reader can no doubt say the English sentence 'Bill likes John' in any number of ways to express not only surprise or anger but many other states as well. ASL on the other hand has no direct correlate with change in pitch, tone of voice, and so on. ASL uses nonmanual behaviors which, like certain types of intonation in speech, simultaneously accompany the lexical string to express such things as a state to be associated with the speaker.

2.6. VERIFICATION

Most of the information on the three nonmanual signals ('mm', 'th', and 'cs') which function as nonmanual adverbs was obtained through examination and study of videotapes of the deaf researchers at the Salk Institute as well as from the intuitions of those same researchers. It seemed important to investigate the generality of the use and interpretation of these nonmanual signals with other signers. If signers from different parts of the country and varied backgrounds gave consistent interpretations to these signals as they occurred in ASL signed sentences, this would bear on the generality of their interpretation. Additionally, if ASL signers generally used these facial signals in adverbial functions (without discussion, prompting, or direct elicitation), this would lend support to the analysis presented here.

The following story was constructed in English, about a day at the beach and an incident that occurred there. It included descriptions of events which might elicit the nonmanual signals discussed here because of the meanings presumed to be coded by them.

At the Beach

I had an awful time yesterday. My friend and I went to the beach hoping to spend the day relaxing and watching the people go by. We put our blankets down in a good place and before long we were getting interested in what was happening around us. There were people playing with a frisbee, others walking around, and even a couple of dogs racing around near the surf. We were both getting a lot of pleasure out of simply watching what was going on.

Wouldn't you know it — some clumsy man walked right in front of us and spilled a whole glass of coke on my friend. He said he was sorry and then walked away as if nothing was wrong. Not only had the coke gotten all over her brand new beautiful swimming suit, but it had also spilled on her towel, which was now wet and sticky. I couldn't keep from laughing — coke was dripping from her hair onto her face. I gave her my towel so she could dry herself off. My friend is not an ordinary girl. If something like that happens to her, she will never be satisfied unless she gets revenge. As she was drying herself off I could see that she was thinking about how she could get even. I started to get an uneasy feeling as she walked over to the refreshment stand because I didn't know what she was going to do — and the man was pretty big.

I looked over to see where the man was but I couldn't find him. I looked back at my friend, who was now placing her order and then I saw him. The man was standing right behind my friend, and she didn't know that he was there! I didn't know what to do. Should I run over and try to let her know? It was too late. She had already bought a big coke. She had obviously seen the man behind her, but she hadn't done anything to him. Now I was getting confused. Is this the same girl that always gets revenge? She had had a chance to pour the coke over the guy's head, but instead she was just walking back towards me. That was when I remembered that more than anything else, she hates to have people laugh at her. I knew it was hopeless to resist so I just sat still while she slowly poured ice-cold coke all over me.

The following sentences were designed to promote the 'mm' signal:

(59)   a. My friend and I went to the beach hoping to spend the day *relaxing and watching* the people go by.
       b. We were both *getting a lot of pleasure out of simply watching* what was going on.
       c. . . . then *walked away as if nothing was wrong.*

These sentences were designed to promote the 'cs' signal:

(60)   a. Not only had the coke gotten all over her *brand new* beautiful swimming suit . . .
       b. The man was *standing right behind my friend.*

These sentences were designed to promote the 'th' signal:

(61)   a. . . . some *clumsy man walked* right in front of us and *spilled* a whole glass of coke on my friend.
       b. . . . *spilled on her towel* . . .

Volunteers from California State University, Northridge, were asked to tell the story in ASL. They were given copies of the story approximately one week in advance. Accompanying the story was an instruction sheet which asked the volunteers to read the story through enough times so that they could remember the events in the story. They were asked not to try to remember the English, but to simply try to remember the *events* in the story. The volunteers were asked to tell the story using American Sign Language. They were asked to simply be themselves and tell the story as if they were telling the story to a friend.

Altogether, ten individuals told the story. Four were involved in ASL research at the Salk Institute (three of the four were native signers), and the other six were volunteers from CSUN (three of the six volunteers were native signers). These individuals had quite varied backgrounds. The following are some of the schools which one or more of these individuals have attended: Illinois School for the Deaf, California School for the Deaf (Berkeley), California School for the Deaf (Riverside), Utah School for the Deaf, Washington State School for the Deaf, American School for the

Deaf (Connecticut), Oregon State School for the Deaf, Indiana School for the Deaf, Gallaudet College, California State University (Northridge), and University of California (San Diego).

Each signer's ASL story was videotaped so that a detailed analysis of both the manual signs and the nonmanual signals could be made.

In telling the story in ASL, some signers used lexical signs to convey meanings such as 'getting a lot of pleasure . . . . ' For example, some of the signers used the sign ENJOY followed by the verb LOOK to convey that meaning without using the nonmanual signal 'mm'. Others used both. For example, one signer, after it was established that he was talking about himself and his friend, produced the following:

m m
<u>   </u>

(62)   ENJOY LOOK-AROUND

where 'mm' was present throughout the verb phrase. Other signers talked about the same situation without using the verb ENJOY:

m m
<u>   </u>

(63)   LOOK-AROUND

The nonmanual adverb 'mm' also showed up in places where I was not expecting it, based on the way the story was created.

m m
<u>   </u>

(64)   SOME PEOPLE WALK TRAFFIC[+]

The sign I have glossed as TRAFFIC[+] is made like the sign TRAFFIC but with the hands oriented so that the back of one of the hands faces the signer. It indicates that people walked back and forth in front of the character in the story.

Thus, for a given signer, the nonmanual adverb 'mm' was not always produced in every situation where it might have been expected to appear. However, every single signer used the nonmanual adverb 'mm' in at least one of the contexts in the story. It is significant that 'mm' was never used with any nouns; it was always used with a single verb or a verb phrase. The nonmanual signal exhibited the rapid onset and offset coinciding with the formation of the verb or verb phrase; it was a distinctly formed, recognizable signal.

It was used at least once with each of the following signs: WALK, LOOK-AROUND, TAKE-IT-EASY ($\emptyset$B$'$B ^{vzv}), ENJOY, REST, GO, LIE-DOWN, and SUNBATHE.

Comparable results were found for the other two nonmanual signals.

Seven of the signers used the 'th' signal. It occurred when the signers were showing liquid dripping from the character's hair, with a 1-classifier showing the approach of the awkward man, with classifiers showing people mingling, and with a form of the sign CARRY (appropriate in form for carrying a bottle). It also did not occur with any nouns.

Six of the signers used the 'cs' signal. It occurred with the adjective NEW, with classifiers showing that one person was behind another person, and with the sign BEHIND ($A'A_T^{>x}$).

In the signed stories other facial behaviors occurred, of course; but it is significant that the particular nonmanual signals studied here were consistently produced by signers in a natural story-telling situation with no prompting. Furthermore, it is significant that the signers produced the nonmanual signals only cooccurring with verbal or adverbial constituents, not with nominal constituents.

In addition to finding out if these individuals would produce these nonmanual signals (given an appropriate situation), I was also interested in finding out how uniformly sequences containing these signals were interpreted. A native signer produced short sentences using these signals, and the six CSUN volunteers were asked to write down what the sentences meant in English.

For example, consider the following string:

$$\overline{\text{th}}$$

MAN FIGURE-OUT[+]. It contains only two signs: MAN and an inflected form of FIGURE-OUT (made with each repetition of the sign lower than the previous one) which is associated with figuring out something from top to bottom (e.g. an income-tax form).

The signers could have merely translated the two signs with something like, 'The man figured something out.' In fact, all six of these signers indicated that either the man was making mistakes or that he was doing it carelessly. The following is typical of the responses: 'Man figures out something without knowing what he is doing.'

When the same string was signed with the 'mm' expression accompanying the verb, none of the signers indicated either carelessness or mistakes. In fact, the signers selected one of the two general interpretations of the 'mm' signal which were mentioned earlier. They said that the man was enjoying himself while he was figuring something out, or they said that the man was figuring things out as a normal state. One of the six apparently deduced from the ease of figuring that the man was a genius. The following response is typical: 'Man just figures it out — as normal state.'

In addition to adverbial signals, one of the strings was accompanied by the nonmanual surprise expression discussed earlier. The string was $\overline{\text{MOTHER COME HOME}}^{\text{'surprise'}}$. Not one of the signers indicated that the mother was surprised. They all indicated that the signer was surprised that mother had come home.

It seems reasonable to conclude from the syntactic analysis presented earlier and the results of the research at CSUN that the use of these signals is very widespread. Not only did these signers from various parts of the country produce these facial signals with no prompting (only the proper context for their use), but their interpretation of them was also uniform.

2.7. SUMMARY

In this chapter we have seen five major roles played by nonmanual behaviors: lexical roles, grammatical markers, pantomime, adverbs, and reflections of emotional states. Many of the behaviors were clearly communicative but did not have obvious linguistic analyses. For example, the most linguistically remote type of nonmanual behavior discussed was pantomimic. No linguistic analysis was presented for these types of behaviors. On the other hand, many of the nonmanual behaviors we looked at formed distinct nonmanual signals which were analyzed as grammatical markers (restrictive relative clauses, topics, and yes–no questions), and adverbs ('mm', 'cs', and 'th'). A particular head nod ('hn'), which is required by certain *syntactic* structures, also provided evidence that it could be viewed as an underlying predicate. We also looked at other communicative signals which were not analyzed as part of the sentence structure but which could be viewed as functioning at the performative level (signals indicating emotional states such as surprise and anger).

Evidence was also provided that the use and interpretation of the nonmanual behaviors discussed in this chapter are not idiosyncratic. Signers from several areas of the country were involved in this research and showed no evidence for distinct regional differences in either use or interpretation.

We have also seen that the distinction between a 'linguistic function' and a 'communicative nonlinguistic function' is a very difficult one. In ASL a broad range of functions is performed by the various nonmanual behaviors. We have seen that a particular combination of facial expression, head position, and body position marks an ASL utterance as a question. Most, if not all, linguists would accept this as a grammatical function: identifying a clause as a question. Another combination of nonmanual behaviors indicates surprise on the part of the signer. Is there any reason *a priori* that this should be any less 'linguistic' than the nonmanual behaviors which indicate that an ASL clause is a question? What about a facial expression that indicates doubt on the part of the signer, excitement, insistence, etc.? For those who feel that these are 'paralinguistic', would they be more 'purely linguistic' if exactly the same function were carried out by a sign? The distinction between 'merely communicative' and 'linguistic' cannot be based on the distinction between the segmental or suprasegmental status of a given signal. Once the suprasegmental door is unlocked to let in things like tone and 'question intonation' in spoken language, one can no longer argue that segmental status is a prerequisite for linguistic status. On what grounds, then, should something be called 'linguistic' as opposed to 'communicative'?

NOTES

1. ASL does not use determiners equivalent to 'a' and 'the' in English. As a result, the gloss shown could have used the determiner 'a' instead of 'the'. The appropriate determiner would depend on context, and possibly other nonmanual behaviors yet to be identified.
2. The notation ($G^{ə\perp}$) is an example of the notation used in Stokoe et al. (1965). I will not provide any explanation of this notation here. The reader is referred to Stokoe et al. for a complete description.
3. For more details on timing, topic marking, and how this relates to the issue of word order in ASL, the reader is referred to 3.3.1.

4. To the best of my knowledge this lack of eye contact during 'role playing' sequences was first discussed by Bendixen (1975). I have used the term 'pantomimic activity' in describing this type of role-playing sequence because the facial expressions used are to be associated with the person whose role is being adopted. The facial expressions shown during the role playing are very important because without them the addressee could be in doubt as to whether any role playing was going on at all. For example, signers would be in doubt as to how to interpret the following:

$$\frac{\overline{\text{'nod'}}}{\text{no eye contact}}$$

BILL   PRO.3 GO MOVIE

The signer would be in doubt as to whether the role playing stopped after 'nod' or not. If the role playing had stopped, then the speaker could be referring to Bill with the sign PRO.3. However, if the role playing had not stopped and the signer is still maintaining the role of Bill, then PRO.3 must refer to someone else.

5. Sometimes the head nod 'hn' occurs only once and sometimes it is repeated. By symbolizing the head nod as 'hn' I do not mean to imply that signers are limited to a single head nod.

6. We will see the same rhetorical use of constituents marked by 'narrow eyes + q' in 2.3.3.

7. The example of 'gapping' presented in the text contains a series of gapped clauses rather than a single gapped clause. I have chosen to illustrate it this way because of the naturalness of the gapping when several clauses are involved. However, this can also be done with a single clause. For example, the following is acceptable to the signers I have discussed this with:

$$\overline{\text{hn}}$$

PRO.1 BRING HOT-DOG; JOHN HAMBURGER

They emphasize, however, that a signer would not stop signing at the end of this string. That is, the string above would appear naturally in a context of a description of a picnic and would be followed by a continued description of what happened, etc. The string does not appear to be natural when viewed in isolation.

8. I presently know of one circumstance where 'hn' does not appear with the repeated pronoun. If a signer is stressing the signs (in a way that appears equivalent to increasing the amplitude of an audio signal) and also has a particular kind of nonneutral facial expression (i.e. angry), the head nod 'hn' does not appear. I have no explanation for this phenomenon.

    In cases where there is an internal head nod, it is stretched out so that it ends with the signing of the repeated pronoun.

9. Stokoe et al. (1965) observe that ASL does not have auxiliary verbs equivalent to 'be' or 'do' in English. ASL does have a couple of signs which translate as 'do'. The first is $\phi\sqrt{C_v}\sqrt{C_v}{}^z$ and is clearly not an auxiliary. It is used as a main verb indicating action, activity, or behavior.

    Battison (1973) claims that the fingerspelled D-O represents a borrowing from English which has become lexicalized as an ASL sign, has several forms, and undergoes regular morphological processes. The sign is also not an auxiliary in ASL.

10. This is not equivalent to the rule of 'do-gobbling' (Ross 1972) which deletes the main verb 'do'.

11. Notice that in addition to the reading of 'The dog did chase the cat' in which there is no contrastive stress on 'did', there is another way of saying this string which does contain contrastive stress on 'did'. This would occur naturally in an argument about whether or not the dog chased the cat, where one person would say something like, 'You are wrong! The dog *did* chase the cat.' Evidently 'do' accepts contrastive stress when existence versus nonexistence is the issue.

12. Part of the nod (the return to a neutral head position) can apparently be suppressed under special circumstances. This was shown to me by Ted Supalla (personal communication). He superimposed a particular facial signal onto the nonmanual signal 'hn' accompanying DOG, and in that case there was a downward movement of the head at the beginning of the sign DOG and the head stayed down during the sign DOG. I interpreted the fact that his head had to go down as a reflection of the presence of 'hn'.

13. Again, I have not been able to uncover any evidence which would shed some light on the nonoccurrence of 'hn' in this environment with stressed signs and special facial expression, etc.

14. The verb-phrase node in these examples is supported by the evidence concerning topicalization. That is, in (40) the verb and object were topicalized together. It would be impossible to topicalize the verb by itself and leave the subject and object behind. Similarly, a time adverbial can appear between the subject and the verb, but not between the verb and the object.

15. Stokoe (1960) mentions a headshake which negates, but the headshake he describes is much smaller than the headshake being described here. In fact, the headshake he describes was small enough to make it easy to overlook in a filmed conversation.

16. This headshake also occurs as an answer to a question, and as a result could precede a sentence which was an echo of the original question. In such a case, the headshake does not negate the following clause, but is interpreted as an answer to the question. This is comparable to the English, 'No, I stayed', or ' "headshake", I stayed.' The 'no' does not negate the following sentence – it answers the preceding question.

17. The notation '[I:continuous]' indicates that the verb is inflected for continuous aspect. In the case of the verb FISH, the out-and-back movement of the citation form of the sign is simply repeated again and again. A verb like DRIVE whose citation form does not have this motion changes its motion to an out-and-back movement and is also repeated when inflected for continuous aspect.

18. What happens when there are conflicting requirements, such as raising and lowering the eyebrows, is a topic which will not be discussed here.

19. There is one other case where this nonmanual signal is present, but its syntactic role is not yet clear. That is, I have seen a few examples like the following:

$$\overline{\rule{3cm}{0pt}\text{head nodding}\rule{5cm}{0pt}}$$
$$\overline{\rule{8cm}{0pt}\text{mm}}\;.$$
JOHN FISH$^{[\text{I:continuous}]}$
'It is a characteristic of John's that he enjoys fishing.'

This example is exceptional in at least two ways. First, the nonmanual signal 'mm' accompanies the entire clause. Second, the head nodding is required. The combination has the interpretation shown. I have not yet gathered enough examples of nonmanual signals being used in this way to be able to present an analysis here.

20. The term 'path of movement' refers to a sign where the hand(s) move from one location to another location. In a 'local movement' the fingers may be wiggling, etc., but the hands don't trace a path in forming the sign.

21. To produce this expression imagine pronouncing 'th' and simultaneously pushing the lips out. The notation 'th' was suggested by Ted Supalla.

22. ASL uses distinct handshapes to represent different types of objects. The erect 1-classifier (index finger pointing up) represents people either standing or walking. If the person is sitting down, a bent-V classifier would be used. This bent-V classifier is also used to represent animals like a dog or a cat. These are discussed in much greater detail in 3.8 and 3.9.

The semicircle in the text represents the 'signing space' in front of the signer. The arrow represents the movement of the 1-classifier.

23. There may also be an interpretation that the engine is running improperly, but in this case the form of the sign generally changes. Instead of being made in one place, the sign moves up and down, or down in steps, and the body also moves forward and backward slightly. When this happens there is no question about the interpretation – the engine is running badly.

24. One way of distinguishing between a pantomimic role-playing sequence and direct quotation (which can also be thought of as a type of pantomimic recreation of an event) appears to be whether the signer adopts a body position, head position, and eye gaze appropriate for speaking to someone. For example, if the signer changes his body orientation to the side with his eye gaze apparently directed at an imaginary signer, this would be interpreted as direct quotation. On the other hand, if the signer does not do this, then direct quotation may not be involved. Ted Supalla has demonstrated for me cases which are clearly one or the other and pointed out things like eye gaze, body orientation, etc. However, I have not examined videotapes of everyday conversation to see if the distinction is always this clear.

3

Word Order

Languages indicate the relationship between a verb and its arguments in different ways. The four arguments in the following
English sentence each have a special syntactic and semantic relation
to the verb 'give'.

(1) Bill gave the book to John in the lobby.

Two of the arguments in this sentence are preceded by prepositions. The preposition 'to' indicates that 'John' is the recipient of
the action. 'The lobby' is the location of the action, indicated by
the preposition 'in'. Two of the arguments, 'Bill' and 'the book',
have no prepositions associated with them, yet their relationship
to the verb is clear. 'Bill' is the subject of the verb and the agent
(the one who does the giving) and 'the book' is the object which
was given. How are these two relationships determined? One possible explanation is that there is only one way to make sense out
of 'Bill', 'the book', and 'gave'. Humans give objects and not the
other way around. It is well known, however, that this is false.
The incorrectness of this explanation can be clearly seen by reversing the order of the arguments in (1) above.

(2) The book gave Bill to John in the lobby.

Exchanging the position of 'the book' and 'Bill' has also exchanged
their syntactic and semantic roles. The book is now the subject
and the agent, while Bill is the object which was given. These two
examples demonstrate the well-known fact that in English the
order of constituents (i.e. word order) is significant in determining
the relationships between a verb and its arguments. We will next

examine whether or not word order has grammatical significance in American Sign Language.

Before presenting any new research, I will first examine the conflicting claims which have been made about word order in ASL.

Fischer (1975) claimed that ASL is now basically an SVO language. She supported this position with the following observations about ASL:

This [SVO] is the order one finds in a sentence with reversible subject and object which are full noun phrases and not 'apposativized' with pronouns. It is also the order one gets in subordinate clauses with *any* two full noun phrases for subject and object. Any other order will have intonation breaks (Fischer 1975: 5).

She also notes that SOV order occurs in the case of 'non-reversible noun phrases and pronouns [which are cliticized to a verb]' (Fischer 1975: 14). By 'reversible subject and object' Fischer says that she means that the subject and object could be reversed and one would still have a semantically plausible utterance. For example, if the positions of 'John' and 'Mary' are exchanged in 'John likes Mary', an acceptable sentence is formed in which 'Mary' is the subject and 'John' is the object: 'Mary likes John.' Thus, in her terms, 'John' and 'Mary' are reversible in the sentence, 'John likes Mary.'

Fischer also argues that the basic word order can be changed by movement rules, and that when this occurs there will be what she called an 'intonation break' between the moved constituent and the rest of the sentence. For example, the object in the sentence DOG CHASE CAT could be topicalized. This would change the word order so that the topicalized object is in initial position and separated from the rest of the sentence by an 'intonation break' (which we shall indicate informally here by a comma).

(3)   CAT, DOG CHASE
      'As for the cat, the dog chased it.'

Similarly, if the verb phrase had been topicalized, the verb and accompanying object would be moved to initial position and separated from the subject by an 'intonation break'. (We will see shortly what the 'intonation break' really is.)

(4)   CHASE CAT, DOG[1]
      'As for chasing the cat, the dog did it.'

To summarize, the following are the different orders and the 'breaks' associated with them:

SVO   This is the underlying order; no breaks.

O,SV   The object has been topicalized and there is a break between it and the rest of the sentence.

VO,S   The verb phrase has been topicalized and there is a break between it and the rest of the sentence. Fischer claims that this order could also be a result of the post-position of the subject.

Notice that in the last three examples the subject appeared in either initial, medial, or final position. The same is true of the verb and object. However, this does not mean that the word order is random. A very simple rule predicts the location of the subject and the object: on either side of the 'intonation break', if the subject or object accompanies the verb, the subject precedes the verb and the object follows the verb. There can never be any confusion between the subject and the object.

Fischer further supported her case for the underlying status of SVO order by claiming that SVO is the order one gets in subordinate clauses with any two full noun phrases for subject and object (1975: 5). She also claims that noun—transitive verb—noun sequences are always interpreted as SVO sequences (1975: 6).

Fischer claims that for non-reversible subject and object (i.e. where only one of two noun phrases is a possible subject, or only one is a possible object, as in 'The man read the newspaper', word order is considerably freer.

What Fischer's claim boils down to is that word order is considerably freer if there is no possibility of confusion based upon the semantics of the lexical items present in a sentence. Men read newspapers, not the other way around. According to Fischer, given the lexical items MAN, READ, and NEWSPAPER and the intention to communicate that the man read the newspaper, the signer could also use SOV order or OVS order in addition to SVO order and those orders derived from it. That is, it should be possible to say

(5)   NEWSPAPER READ MAN
      'The man read the newspaper.'

This conflicts with another claim she makes that all noun—transitive verb—noun sequences are interpreted as SVO. NEWS-PAPER READ MAN is clearly a noun–transitive verb–noun sequence, but it is not interpreted as a subject–verb–object sequence. Clearly, only one of the two claims can be correct. It cannot be true that all noun—transitive verb—noun sequences are interpreted as subject–verb–object, and also be true that OVS order is possible. The former claim appears to be true and the latter false.

I have been unable to find any signer who was willing to say that a sequence like (5) (i.e. an object–verb–subject sequence) was something that he would be willing to say. When I asked what a sequence like (5) means, some signers indicated that they *guessed* that it means that a man read a newspaper. This response does not mean that the sequence is grammatical, but simply that some signers are willing, at the request of a linguist, to assign a meaning to a sequence that would not be used by them.

I have also been unable to find any OVS sequence in a more natural situation such as conversation or a monologue.

Fischer makes one other claim about SOV order. She claims that in addition to being used for nonreversible subject and object, it can also be used if the direction or orientation of the verb indicates the grammatical relations involved (cf. Lacy 1974; Fischer 1975; Friedman 1976).[2]

To summarize, according to Fischer the following orders are grammatical in ASL:

SVO This is the underlying order.

O,SV Topicalized object.

VO,S Topicalized verb phrase or postposed subject.

SOV 'Nonreversible subject and object' or grammatical relations shown by the direction or orientation of the verb.

OVS 'Nonreversible subject and object'. (Evidence indicates that OVS order is ungrammatical.)

Friedman (1976) has some very different views on word order in ASL:

Word order is relatively free, with the exception of the tendency for the verb to be last (1976: 142).

Nominal lexical items may appear on the surface after their spatial establishment seemingly wherever they please (1976: 142).

These mechanisms have either been developed because of or have resulted in a lack of fixed word order in the language (1976: 145).

Friedman's findings contradict the findings of Fischer. Friedman sees word order as playing no role in the grammar of ASL − the relations between a verb and its arguments being determined by other mechanisms or by context.

Recall that Fischer observed that several orders of subject, verb, and object occur in ASL. Fischer claimed that SVO order was underlying and the O,VS and VO,S orders were derived from it. She also claimed that SOV and OVS orders were possible given special semantically determined circumstances. The main point is that − with the exception of these last two orders − the word order itself, and the accompanying 'intonation breaks', provide sufficient information for determining the subject and object.

Friedman also observes that several word orders occur, but denies that there is any grammatical significance to word order. She does not justify this claim by providing examples of nonpredictable variation in the orders of subject and object. In fact, she provides no justification at all.

Friedman is apparently bothered by the fact that English also uses subject–verb–object order. For example, she discusses an example from Edge and Herrmann (1975). She states that they used nonverbal skits with an informant, and then asked the informant to describe the skit using two name signs and a desired verb. They found that under these circumstances the informant invariably formed a sentence using SVO order (i.e. LEORA BOTHER VICKI). This is exactly what you would expect given Fischer's claims about word order. However, they claim that this may not be support for Fischer's claim because it may be a reflection of the fact that the signer knows English and is following the English order. They lengthened their skits and asked their informant to use the desired verb sign at some point in the description of the skit, and they found that in this more extended description not all the NP arguments showed up explicitly in the surface form of the sentences produced.

They found, for example, that the object could be eliminated from the sentences, leaving presumably the subject and the verb, in that order. This certainly provides no evidence against Fischer's claim. In fact, it provides support for her claim. If the object is deleted from an SVO sentence, a subject and a verb should be left and they should be in subject–verb order. Friedman does not view the data in this way. She apparently feels that since the subject–verb–object sentences do not show up in more extended discourse, they must not be a normal type of ASL sentence. This completely misses the point. Fischer's claim is that the basic word order in ASL is subject–verb–object. This does not mean that every sentence must be in that order. Let us consider the example, LEORA BOTHER VICKI, in more detail. If the signer has a way of indicating the object of BOTHER on the verb itself by changing the direction of the verb, then there is no need to mention VICKI. The fact that VICKI is not mentioned by the signer does not pose any problems for the addressee because the object of the verb is apparent. Does this mean that word order is not significant for determining subject and object? Not at all. To determine the significance of word order, you must look at the orders that do occur. That is, if the subject is mentioned with the verb BOTHER, regardless of whether or not the verb indicates its object, where is the subject placed? If the subject is placed after the verb, that would constitute evidence against Fischer's claim (provided there were no special reason for that placement). However, if the subject is placed before the verb, given no topicalization, etc., this would support Fischer's claim. In fact, the subject is placed before the verb in the unmarked case. Thus, Edge and Herrmann's example supports the claim that ASL is basically an SVO language.

Friedman also discusses role playing, where it is possible for the signer to take the role of one of the principals in a story. She is once again trying to show that the subject and/or the object do not always show up as separate lexical items. Since this is not relevant to the point, I will not review her discussion of role playing. Finally, for some reason Friedman claims that subject–verb–object word order is 'possibly ambiguous' (1976: 132). Once again she provides no evidence for this claim. In fact, she gives no clue as to what this ambiguity might be. In the sequence LEORA BOTHER VICKI there is no doubt that LEORA is the subject and that VICKI is the object. Edge and Herrmann make it clear that the signer, in describing the skits, *invariably* used subject–verb–object order when both the subject and the object appear as separate lexical items. Since Friedman gives no explanation as to what the ambiguity might be, and since I am unable to discover any ambiguity, I see no reason to call SVO sequences 'possibly ambiguous'.

Friedman also discusses deletion and its effect on word order. This is the only grammatical operation she discusses with respect to word order. Friedman analyzes certain object–verb constructions and the possible underlying structures from which they might have been derived. In such object–verb constructions, Friedman argues that the underlying subject must have been deleted. However, she does not argue for the location of the underlying subject but simply decides that the underlying subject must have been initial, and thus finds support for an underlying subject-object-verb order (1976: 136). She next takes up subject–verb-object-verb constructions:

> (6)   PRO.1 PACK CLOTHES PACK FINISH
>   'I packed my clothes.'

She notes that there are several possible ways to look at the data and arbitrarily concludes, apparently on the basis of having found 'evidence' for SOV constructions above, that the underlying order must have been SV+SOV. By deleting the second subject, which is identical to the first, the SVOV construction could be derived. Needless to say, the conclusions Friedman has drawn are entirely unjustified by the evidence she presents. This would be true even if Friedman were arguing that ASL has underlying structures in which order is significant. She is not. Her position is that ASL has no fixed word order. Yet, she is willing to argue that a specific surface structure in which deletion has apparently taken place has been derived from an underlying structure in which order is significant. She argues for underlying order and the lack of it at the same time.

3.1. NOUN–TRANSITIVE VERB–NOUN SEQUENCES

The first question we will attempt to answer is whether or not the word order itself has any significance in the interpretation of ASL sentences.

> (7)   JOHN KICK DOG

This sentence can be signed in at least two different ways. In the first, the relationship between JOHN, DOG, and KICK can be indicated by the direction of the verb. That is, JOHN could be signed on the right, KICK could be signed from right to left, and DOG could be signed on the left. Since KICK began on the side where John was signed and ended on the side where DOG was subsequently signed, the sentence is interpreted to mean that John kicked the dog. One could argue that since the locations established for the nouns and the direction of the verb indicate that John kicked the dog, the word order is not significant. However, locations need not be established for the nouns, and the verb need not be used directionally.

The second way to sign sentence (7) is to make all three signs in 'neutral space'. When this is done, the direction of the verb provides no information about the relationships between JOHN, DOG, and KICK. In spite of this, the interpretation is still that John kicked the dog.

In the first case someone might claim that the directionality determines the interpretation of the sentence, not the word order. That is, the order is just accidental. It could have been any other order. In fact, this is the view of ASL which Friedman presents. In the second case, where directionality plays no role, she would be forced to say that the interpretation depends on the semantics of the individual lexical items rather than on a rule of grammar. In other words the addressee thinks about John, the dog, and kicking, and then takes a guess: John kicked the dog, the dog kicked John, John and the dog were kicked by someone, John and the dog kicked each other, etc. The problem with this view is that in spite of the large number of possibilities *all* signers will agree that John did the kicking and the dog was kicked. This would be an odd result if the interpretation were really a matter of guesswork. That this interpretation is obligatory is shown by reversing the order of JOHN and DOG:

(8)   DOG KICK JOHN
      'The dog kicked John.'

If the signers were really guessing, the interpretation should be the same regardless of the order. It is not. The obvious and straightforward conclusion is that word order is significant.

Recall that Friedman accepts the suggestion of Edge and Herrmann that these SVO sentences may be a reflection of the fact that the informant knows English. However, in a different context, Friedman provides a clear SVO example of her own where she does not question any influence of English.

> (9)   PRO.2 KNOW LYNN?
>   'Do you know Lynn?'

Friedman glosses this as shown above. According to her conception of ASL, which claims no grammatical significance to word order, this could just as easily mean a number of other things. It does not. It is unambiguously SVO. How does a theory like Friedman's explain that the sentences above mean what they do? It cannot, of course. Noun–transitive verb–noun sequences are interpreted as SVO just as Fischer has claimed.

3.2. WORD ORDER AND YES–NO QUESTIONS

Here we will take another look at the nonmanual signal used in forming yes–no questions. The form of an ASL yes–no question is shown in Plate 20. The question being asked is, 'Did the woman forget the purse?', and consists of the three signs in the order shown in (10).

| WOMAN | FORGET | PURSE |

Plate 20.

(10) $\overline{\text{WOMAN FORGET PURSE}}^{\text{q}}$
'Did the woman forget the purse?'

Notice that the order in this question is subject–verb–object. This is not just one of many possible alternative ways of asking this question. This is the only order that is allowed in which all three signs form the question with the intended reading (i.e. 'Did the woman forget the purse?'). All the following sentences are un-grammatical single questions with the intended reading (the aste-risk is used to mark ungrammatical constructions):

(11)   * $\overline{\text{WOMAN PURSE FORGET}}^{\text{q}}$

       * $\overline{\text{PURSE WOMAN FORGET}}^{\text{q}}$

       * $\overline{\text{FORGET WOMAN PURSE}}^{\text{q}}$

       * $\overline{\text{FORGET PURSE WOMAN}}^{\text{q}}$

       * $\overline{\text{PURSE FORGET WOMAN}}^{\text{q}}$

The qualification 'single questions' is necessary here because a sequence like

(12) $\overline{\text{FORGET PURSE}}^{\text{q}}\ \overline{\text{WOMAN}}^{\text{q}}$
'Did she forget the purse? Do you mean the woman?'

is possible; however, it is clearly not a single question.[3]

The fact that this yes–no question, 'Did $\left\{{}^{\text{a}}_{\text{the}}\right\}$ woman forget $\left\{{}^{\text{a}}_{\text{the}}\right\}$ purse?', can only be asked in subject–verb–object order strongly suggests that the underlying order in ASL is subject–verb–object.

3.3. SVO and S,VO ORDER

3.3.0. 'Intonation breaks'

Fischer's claim that SVO was basic was based in part on the

observation that 'any other order will have intonation breaks' (1975: 5). Under the heading of 'intonation breaks' she included 'pauses, head tilts, raising of eyebrows, and/or probably numerous other clues that I as a non-native, non-deaf signer have yet to learn to pay attention to' (1975: 6).

Her claim about the distribution of 'intonation breaks' is not completely accurate. Many sentences with SOV order are exceptions to this claim since they have no 'breaks' of any kind that I can detect.

Secondly, while SVO order does not *require* a 'break', there may be one. The significance of this will be discussed later.

3.3.1. Topicalization

If SVO order occurs, there need not be a break between the subject and what follows. On the other hand, there can be a 'break' between the subject and the rest of the sentence (illustrated in Plate 21) if the subject has been topicalized.

In Plate 21 the subject of the sentence has been topicalized. An appropriate translation of the sentence shown would be, 'As for the dog, it chased the cat.' This example differs in timing, head position, and facial expression from an SVO sentence in which the subject is not topicalized (cf. 2.2.4).

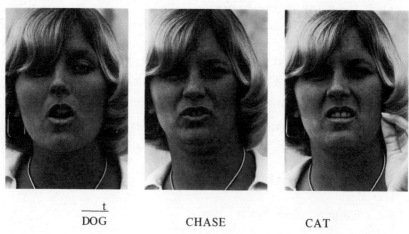

    <u> t </u>

DOG   CHASE   CAT

Plate 21.

3.3.1.1. Timing. The duration of a sign in ASL varies considerably depending on several factors. One of these factors is position within a sentence. I have found that the duration of a sign is least if the sign is in medial position. In comparison with medial position, signs which were initial, but not topics, were held roughly 0.18 seconds (11 VTR fields) longer than the same sign would be held in medial position.[4] Final signs were held roughly 0.28 seconds (17 VTR fields) longer than medial position. Topics were held longer than any other signs that I measured. They were held roughly 0.37 seconds (22 VTR fields) longer than medial position.

Timing a sign involves measuring the interval between the beginning of the sign and the end of the sign. For the most part, it is not too difficult to find these two endpoints. A sign like CAT, when viewed field by field on videotape, has a fairly clear beginning. That is, the hand approaching the head slows down so that the image on the videotape is no longer blurred. The F handshape is also definite before the hand makes contact with the head. I take this to be the beginning of the sign. I count any change away from the F handshape to mean that the sign is over.

This timing data was gotten from sentences produced in isolation and videotaped. There was a lot of variation in the data within groups (i.e. medial signs, final signs, etc.), and only a limited number of signs were timed. As a result this data should only be regarded as indicating a tendency.[5]

3.3.1.2. Facial expression and head position. We are now in a position to distinguish between a question and a topic. The facial expression and head position which accompany the sign DOG in

the sentence, $\overline{\text{DOG}}^{\text{t}}$ CHASE CAT (Plate 21) are distinct from the

facial expression and head position which accompany questions. The two are compared side by side in Plate 22. Notice that the head position is different in the two pictures. For the topic the head is tilted back slightly, with the brows raised slightly. For the question the head is not tilted back, and the body is forward. I have found no evidence that the degree of the brow raise is significant in distinguishing one marker from the other, or even for distinguishing the presence of one of the signals from the lack of it, as long as there is a perceptible raising of the brows. The distinction between the two is in the position of the head and body.

$$\overline{\text{a. DOG}}^{\,t} \qquad\qquad \overline{\text{b. DOG}}^{\,q}$$

Plate 22.

If the head is tilted back, as in Plate 22a, a topic is being marked. If the head is forward, as in Plate 22b, (with or without any forward position of the body), a question is being asked.

We can now distinguish between the ASL sentences which correspond to the following two English sentences:

'The dog?, it chased the cat.'

'As for the dog, it chased the cat.'

In the former, the sign DOG alone will have the facial expression and head (and body) position for a question. In the latter, the sign DOG will be accompanied by the facial expression and head position for a topic. In both cases, the questioned or topicalized sign will be held longer than it could normally be held.

It should now be clear what the 'intonation break' that Fischer reported consists of. The break consists of the sharp change between the facial expression and the head position we have illustrated which mark topics and the facial expression and head position which are used during the rest of the sentence. This, combined with the extra-long duration of the topicalized sign(s), would definitely give the impression of a break between the topic and the following clause.

I should point out that the view of topicalization presented here, apart from the distinction just made between topicalization and questioning, is at odds with a claim made by Friedman, who claimed that the first sign in an utterance is always the topic. This will be discussed in more detail later.

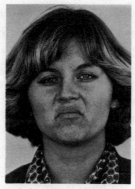

'n' facial expression

Plate 23.

3.3.2. Headshake negation

We will once again be discussing the negating headshake 'n' discussed earlier in 2.3.3. Recall that the headshake is accompanied by a nonneutral facial expression. A facial expression which, if combined with a side-to-side headshake, will form a negating signal is illustrated in Plate 23.

It is important to point out that the negative headshake will not change the polarity of a sentence which contains lexical negation (WOMAN NOT FORGET PURSE), but will reinforce the negativity of the sentence.

The negative headshake accompanies the entire clause that it negates, not just part of it. This is demonstrated by the ungrammaticality of the following example.

(13)   *   WOMAN FORGET PURSE
$$\overline{\qquad\qquad n\qquad}$$

Now let us examine what happens when the negative headshake accompanies an SVO sentence without topic marking on the subject, and the same sequence of signs with topic marking on the subject. Recall that 'n' represents the presence of the side-to-side headshake and a particular facial expression (illustrated in Plate 23).

(14)   DOG CHASE CAT
'It is not the case that the dog chased the cat.'

(15)   DOG CHASE CAT
'As for the dog, it didn't chase the cat.'

The two examples differ with respect to which signs are accompanied by the headshake negation. In the first example, the entire sequence is accompanied by the headshake negation. In the second, however, the topic is not accompanied by the headshake negation. Exactly those signs which are accompanied by the headshake negation fall under its scope. This can be seen clearly by examining the English translations of the two ASL utterances. In the first example, the entire sentence falls under the scope of the negation – 'It is not the case that the dog chased the cat.' The second example is different; DOG is not subject to the negation – 'As for the dog, it didn't chase the cat.'

This suggests that the traditional analysis of topicalization, Chomsky-adjunction of the topicalized constituent to the main clause, is the proper analysis in this case. We will tentatively analyze the negative headshake as a higher verb which takes the clause as its subject.

(16)

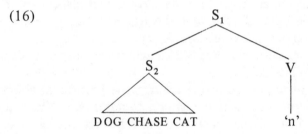

The diagram above underlies the sentence $\overline{\text{DOG CHASE CAT}}^{\text{n}}$. In this case where there is no topic, all the elements in the lower clause fall within the scope of 'n', since 'n' commands all the signs in S_2. However, when a sign is topicalized and Chomsky-adjoined to S_1, it is no longer commanded by 'n'.

(17)

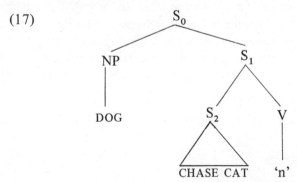

The very important concept 'command' was first introduced into linguistics by Langacker (1966). To determine if one element commands another, simply trace up the tree structure until an S node is reached. If it is possible to trace *down* from that S node to the other element, the first element commands the second.

(18)

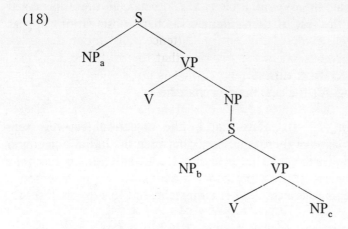

Using the criteria mentioned above, it can be seen clearly that NP_a commands both NP_b and NP_c. Neither of these two NPs commands NP_a, NP_b command NP_c, and NP_c also commands NP_b.

The significance of this concept for ASL is that any element that is commanded by 'n' is subject to its negating force. Thus, where the subject has been topicalized, it is no longer commanded by 'n' and does not fall under the scope of the negation.

(19)

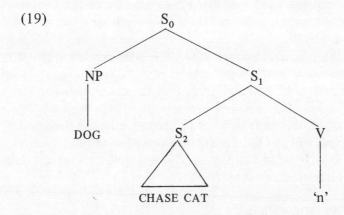

'As for the dog, it didn't chase the cat.'

3.4. O,SV AND VO,S ORDER

We can now look at O,SV and VO,S sentences in light of what has been claimed about topics. Fischer claimed that O,SV order was derived from SVO order by a rule of topicalization. She also claimed that there would be a break between the topicalized object and the rest of the sentence. Fischer's observations appear to be correct.

(20) $\overline{\text{CAT}}^{\;\;\text{t}}$ DOG CHASE
       'As for the cat, the dog chased it.'

Friedman (1976) claims that in the object–subject–verb sentences she has seen there is no break between the initial object and the following subject. This is a direct contradiction to Fischer's claim. However, in the same paper, Friedman presents a sentence which appears to contradict her own claim and to support Fischer.

(21)   GIRL PRO.3[to right] /PRO.3[to left] WANT

       MEET [marker on left makes contact with GIRL marker at right location]

The symbol '/' between the initial object and the following subject is Friedman's notation for a pause. Her discussion of this sentence does not include any information about the type of nonmanual signals we have been discussing, so we have no way of knowing whether or not the head was tilted back slightly or the eyebrows were raised. However, even in Friedman's terms, the pause would constitute a 'break'.

The breaks Fischer observed in O,VS sentences were apparently the extra duration of the topic combined with the change in facial expression and head position from that indicating topic to some other expression. Our analysis predicts that if the negative headshake is present, the topic will not be accompanied by the negative headshake and will not fall under the scope of negation.

This is exactly what happens, and it is parallel to the previous example of a topicalized subject.

(22) $\overline{\text{CAT}}^{\;\;\text{t}}\ \overline{\text{DOG CHASE}}^{\;\;\text{n}}$
       'As for the cat, the dog didn't chase it.'

The resulting structure is also parallel to that for the topicalized subject.

(23)

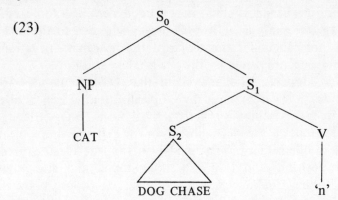

Recall that if a sentence is in SVO order, the subject may or may not be a topic, depending on the timing and the nonmanual signal which accompanies the subject. If the subject is not a topic, the headshake negation will accompany the entire clause. If the subject is also a topic, the headshake negation accompanies all the signs but the subject. As a result, the first sign may or may not be accompanied by the headshake negation, depending on whether or not it is a topic.

The same is not true in the case of a topicalized object. This is demonstrated by the ungrammaticality of the following example:

$$\overline{\qquad\qquad\text{n}\qquad}$$

(24) *   CAT DOG CHASE
        'It isn't the case that the dog chased the cat.'

What can we conclude from the ungrammaticality of this example? First, if word order were free, example (24) should be just as acceptable as the following grammatical example:

$$\overline{\qquad\qquad\text{n}\qquad}$$

(25)   DOG CHASE CAT
        'It isn't the case that the dog chased the cat.'

All the signers I have asked about the grammaticality of a string like (24)

$$\overline{\qquad\qquad\text{n}\qquad}$$

(24) *   CAT DOG CHASE
        'It is not the case that the dog chased the cat.'

unhesitatingly judge it as ungrammatical. The second conclusion, related to the first, is that the object is in initial position because it has been topicalized. As such, it will be marked as a topic, and according to our analysis will be Chomsky-adjoined to the main clause, will not fall under the scope of the headshake negation, and will not be accompanied by the headshake negation.

This data supports Fischer's claim that O,SV sentences are derived from SVO sentences by topicalization. Fischer also claimed that VO,S sentences were derived from SVO sentences by topicalization of the verb phrase or by moving the subject to the end of the sentence. The evidence from the facial expression, head position, and timing marking topics and also what happens with headshake negation will help us choose between these two alternatives. First, in VO,S sentences the verb phrase is marked with the topic signal, 't'.

<pre>
               t   hn
</pre>
(26)   CHASE CAT DOG
'As for chasing the cat, the dog did it.'

(Recall from 2.3.1.4 that 'hn' represents a specific head nod.) What happens in the negative case is as would be predicted.

<pre>
               t   n
</pre>
(27)   CHASE CAT DOG
'As for chasing the cat, the dog didn't do it.'

The symbols 't' and 'n' were introduced earlier in the text. Let me emphasize again that these symbols stand for specific nonmanual activities. 't' indicates that the head is tilted back slightly with the eyebrows raised, and 'n' indicates the presence of a side-to-side headshake accompanied by a particular non-neutral facial expression.

Once again, the topic is separate from the main clause, and the headshake negation accompanies all the signs except the topic. In this case there is only one sign left in the main clause — the subject. While there is no lexical verb left in the main clause, the sign DOG is accompanied by the nonmanual signal we are tentatively analyzing as a negating predicate — 'n'.

This is parallel to the nonnegative case where the verb phrase has been topicalized (section 2.3.1.4). There, the subject was accompanied by a specific up-and-down head movement, 'hn'.

As was the case with the object appearing in initial position, when the verb phrase appears in initial position, ahead of the subject, it must also be marked as the topic. This requirement is illustrated by the ungrammaticality of the following example.

(28) * $\overline{\text{CHASE CAT DOG}}^{\text{n}}$
     'It is not the case that the dog chased the cat.'

This data presents the same picture as before. It supports the claim that VO,S order is derived by topicalization from SVO order. The topic may not be accompanied by the negative headshake and thereby fall under the scope of negation, though the 'comment' (what is predicated of the topic) can be. With this background let us now examine another claim made by Friedman.

3.5. INDEFINITE TOPICS

Friedman suggests that 'it is impossible (or at least difficult) to have an indefinite object as such in ASL (that is, to distinguish an indefinite from a definite)' (1976: 144). This is based on data similar to

. (29) $\overline{\text{GIRL}}^{\text{t}}$ PRO.1 WANT MEET
     'As for the girl, I want to meet her.'

where there is no reading with GIRL taken as indefinite. Further, because of the acceptability of sentences like

(30) SOMEONE GIVE$^{[\text{X: pro.1}]}$ BOOK[6]
     'Somebody gave me a book.'

she would be forced, given her definition of topic (the first sign in an utterance is the topic), to conclude that ASL does allow indefinite topics, though it disallows indefinite objects.

Notice that in (30) SOMEONE is not marked by the nonmanual signal 't'. Our analysis predicts that the entire string could be accompanied by the negative headshake 'n'.

$$\overline{\phantom{\text{SOMEONE GIVE X pro.1 BOO}}}^{\text{n}}$$

(31)   SOMEONE GIVE[X: pro.1] BOOK
'It is not the case that someone gave me a book.'

In this example SOMEONE is not marked as the topic and is accompanied by the headshake negation. The following example, where SOMEONE is marked as a topic and is not accompanied by the headshake negation, is completely unacceptable.

$$\overline{\phantom{\text{SOME}}}^{\text{t}}\overline{\phantom{\text{ONE GIVE X pro.1 BOOK}}}^{\text{n}}$$

(32)   *   SOMEONE GIVE[X: pro.1] BOOK
'As for someone, he didn't give me a book.'

Further, ASL *does* allow indefinite objects. Examples with indefinite objects are easy to find.

(33)   PRO.1 FORGET SOMETHING
'I forgot something.'

This data suggests that rather than a prohibition against indefinite objects, ASL has a prohibition against indefinite topics. This is to be expected on semantic, pragmatic grounds.

3.6. SUBJECT–OBJECT–VERB ORDER: COMPLICATIONS DUE TO ICONICITY AND OTHER MIMETIC DEVICES IN ASL

I have purposely put off discussion of SOV order because strong feelings about the grammaticality of sentences with this order of constituents are generally lacking. However, the fact that some examples are presented as grammatical and others aren't does represent a genuine difference in acceptability.

Recall that this is the order which Fischer claimed was used with 'nonreversible subject and object'. What she means is that a noun–noun–verb sequence which only makes sense if the first noun is the subject and the second noun is the object will be so interpreted. The sentence

(34)   MAN BOOK READ
'The man read the book.'

has only one sensible interpretation — the one shown. However, there are many sentences which only make sense if they are interpreted as SOV, yet they are unacceptable to my informants. The following examples are typical:

(35) a. * MAN MOVIE SEE
      b. * MAN NUMBER FORGET
      c. * BOY CANDY NOT LIKE

If Fischer's claim is correct, all the above sentences should be grammatical. Since they are not, we will attempt to discover the reason for their lack of acceptability.

One way of getting at this problem would be to make a list of acceptable and unacceptable sentences and to compare them to attempt to discover what it is about the unacceptable ones that makes them unacceptable. In fact, there is an easier way to get at this problem. There are SOV sequences which must be signed in a certain way in order for that sequence to be acceptable. If the same sequence of signs is signed in a different way, it is less acceptable. The sentence WOMAN PIE PUT-IN-OVEN is just such a sequence. There is a right way and a wrong way to produce this string. For this sequence to be acceptable, the hand which is used as the base hand for PIE is used as the active hand for the sign PUT-IN-OVEN. At first, this may seem like a strange requirement, but it has the following effect on the 'picture' that is presented to the addressee. The base hand for the sign PIE is a flat open hand, palm up. After the sign PIE is made, the base hand is in exactly the position it would be in if it were holding a real pie. In the acceptable version of the string WOMAN PIE PUT-IN-OVEN, it is exactly this hand, the one which could be imagined as holding a pie, which is used as the active hand for the sign PUT-IN-OVEN. As a result, the hand which could be imagined as holding a pie can now be imagined as putting that pie in the oven.

The same sequence of three signs is unacceptable to my informants if the base hand for the sign PIE is not used as the active hand for the sign PUT-IN-OVEN. This is apparently because the hand which could be imagined as holding the pie is not subsequently used to 'put the pie in the oven'. It seems that the iconicity of the sequence is important for this SOV sequence.[7]

In the following SOV sequence, iconicity is also important. The sequence ME BICYCLE BUY is acceptable if the signer, during the sign BICYCLE, gazes to a point on his left, for example. This establishes the bicycle, for grammatical purposes, on the signer's left. The last sign BUY is then directed toward the left, indicating that the object of BUY is the bicycle.

If the three signs are made in citation form and without the use of eye gaze during the sign BICYCLE, the sequence is unacceptable to my informants.

In both the acceptable versions, the relationships between the verb and its arguments are represented in some way. In the first example, the relationship between the pie and the oven was shown iconically, in that one hand could be imagined as holding a pie and then putting it in an oven. In the second example, the establishment of a locus for BICYCLE and the directionality of the verb indicated the relationship between the verb BUY and the noun BICYCLE. In both the unacceptable versions, the relationship between the verbs and their arguments was not shown.

We will now return to the original example MAN BOOK READ. Recall that this is an acceptable sentence. The thing which apparently makes this sequence acceptable is the fact that after the sign BOOK is made, one of the hands which was used to make the sign is left behind and can be imagined as holding a book (or representing the book itself). Next, the sign READ is directed at that same hand, thus indicating through the use of the directional verb READ the relationship between the verb and its object.

Compare this with the sequence MAN BOOK BUY which, without the use of eye gaze and directionality of the verb BUY, is unacceptable. The reason that this sequence is unacceptable appears to be that even though the hand used to make the sign BOOK can be imagined as holding a book, this is not enough to establish a location which a directional verb like BUY can grammatically refer to.

This is admittedly very vague; however, it appears to be what is responsible for the difference between an acceptable and an unacceptable SOV sequence. In none of the unacceptable SOV sequences, including those in (35),

(35)   a. * MAN MOVIE SEE
      b. * MAN NUMBER FORGET
      c. * BOY CANDY NOT LIKE

can I see a way to analyze them as indicating the relationships between the verb and its object in some way. In the sentence * MAN MOVIE SEE, even though the verb SEE is able to indicate its object by being directed toward a grammatically established locus, there is no locus which the sign can be directed at. Movies cannot be held in the palm, nor are they generally seen on the palm, hence the unacceptability of that sequence. However, this sequence becomes acceptable if, during the sign MOVIE, the signer raises his eye gaze as if looking at a movie screen, and then directs the sign SEE at that location. The verb FORGET in the next example is not a directional verb in the first place and therefore could not show its relationship to the noun NUMBER. There is also no relationship between CANDY and LIKE which can be seen in the form of the signs.

If this is correct, then the SOV order itself does not give any information about the grammatical relationships. As we have seen, however, unless the sequence does include information about the relationship between the activity and the object involved in some spatial, pictorial sense, the sequence will be unacceptable. There may, in fact, be a continuum here between the acceptable sentences, in which the relationship between the verb and the object is clearly shown, and the unacceptable sentences, where it is not shown at all. Judgments as to the grammaticality of these sentences would vary depending on where the sentence fell on the continuum (i.e. how well the relationship between the verb and the object is depicted).

3.7. A POSSIBLE EXCEPTION

If a signer wishes to say that John hit a ball with a bat, he might produce the following sentence.

(36)   BALL JOHN SWING-A-BAT

Ted Supalla first pointed this example out to me as an example of a sequence where SVO order is unacceptable and where an initial object is not marked as a topic. As such it should be carefully examined.

The sign SWING-A-BAT is made with both hands in a configuration appropriate for holding a baseball bat (except that the fists are closed). The sign begins with the hands near one shoulder (as if the bat were ready to be swung), then both hands move as if they were swinging the bat and stop when the hands are in front of the body.

In addition to the fact that BALL need not be marked as the topic, there is one other difference between BALL JOHN SWING-A-

$$\overline{}^{t}$$

BAT and a sentence like CAR JOHN BUY (where CAR must be marked as the topic or the sequence is not well formed). If the sign BUY is accompanied by the nonmanual adverb 'th', the sentence is interpreted to mean that it was stupid of John to buy the car — he may have been gullible and believed everything that the used-car salesman told him, etc. In spite of this, he bought the car.

If the same nonmanual signal 'th' accompanies the sign SWING-A-BAT, the sentence can be interpreted to mean that John *missed* the ball. The nonmanual adverb seems to have changed the meaning of the sentence completely. Instead of meaning 'hit the ball with a bat', the interpretation is 'swing the bat and miss the ball'.

The verb SWING-A-BAT is operating differently from the verbs we have discussed so far. Unless there is some indication to the contrary (i.e. the nonmanual signal 'th'), there is an implication that contact was made with the ball. However, if there is some indication to the contrary, then it is interpreted as if no contact was made with the ball. This is quite different from a verb like BUY. In the sentence

(37) $\overline{}^{t}$
CAR JOHN BUY
'As for the car, John bought it.'

there can never be any question about whether or not the car was bought. If CAR is the object of BUY, and it is in the example above, then the car was bought. It may have been bought foolishly, eagerly, with apprehension, etc., but it was bought.

I do not have a good explanation for the behavior of the verb SWING-A-BAT, but it may be possible to analyze it in a way similar to the analysis in one of the next three sections (cf. in particular 3.10).

3.8. CLASSIFIERS AND WORD ORDER

3.8.1. Locatives and actions

Earlier it was argued that underlyingly objects are postverbal but could be moved to initial position by topicalization. When this is done, the topicalized object is marked as the topic both by the extended duration of the sign and by the head position and facial expression which are present throughout the signing of the topic.

The constructions we will be discussing in this section have a normal word order which is not subject–verb–object. Further, the initial sign in many of these sentences appears at first glance to be an object which is not marked as the topic of the sentence. The existence of a class of sentence types which has a normal order of object–subject–verb with no topic marking on the initial object could have a number of implications, depending on the analysis of the sentences. We will first take a closer look at the data.

Plate 24 illustrates a typical example of a sentence of the type discussed above. It is roughly equivalent to the English sentence, 'A cat is lying on the fence.'

FENCE   4–CL——————————————————————————

CAT   V̈–CL on 4–CL

Plate 24.

There are several comments to make about the sign sequence shown in Plate 24. First, it is clear that there is no topic marking on the sign FENCE. This does not mean that in this type of sentence the initial sign could not be marked as topic, rather that it need not be marked as topic. I am assuming that if a sign is not marked by the signal 't', this is because it is not a topic.

Second, the sign FENCE is followed by a classifier which represents physical objects with a specific shape. I have called the classifier a 4-classifier, 4-CL, because it uses the handshape of the ASL number four. The 4-classifier used in the example above could be used to represent not only a fence, but a wall, a hedge, etc. All of these have the general characteristics of being something like an erect rectangular 'plate', that may or may not be completely solid (i.e. there could be spaces in a fence, depending on the type of fence; there are not generally spaces in a brick wall).

Third, this 4-classifier (made with one hand) remains throughout the rest of the signs (which are articulated with the other hand) though we will see examples later where this does not occur. The presence and duration of the classifier is indicated by the line which follows the 4-classifier in the transcription.

Fourth, the sign CAT is also followed by a classifier. I have called the classifier used in the third photograph 'V̈–CL' because it uses the bent-V (V̈) handshape. This particular classifier is used to represent some animals and humans with their legs bent.

Fifth, the relationship between the cat and the fence under discussion is not shown by a lexical sign like ON. Instead, the relationship between the cat and the fence is shown in the final picture, where the two classifiers are placed in a spatial relationship to one another. By placing the bent-V classifier on top of the 4-classifier, the signer indicates that the cat was on the fence. This is apparently the 'neutral' way to indicate that a cat is on a fence. That is, this configuration does not necessarily indicate the orientation of the cat with respect to the fence. However, the lack of motion of the bent-V classifier indicates that the cat was still rather than in motion. It is easy to see that there is a lot of information packed into the orientation, location, and (lack of) movement of the two classifiers.[8]

Plates 25, 26, and 27 will give a much clearer picture of the kind of information which these classifier predicates communicate. In each case there is a different relationship holding between the cat and the fence.

In Plate 25 (which only shows the relationship between the classifiers) the cat is interpreted as lying 'stomach down' on the

V̈-CL on 4-CL

Plate 25.

fence and parallel to it because of the orientation of the bent-V classifier on the 4-classifier. Once again, since there is no movement of the classifiers, the interpretation is that there was no actual movement.

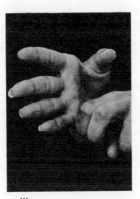

V̈-CL beside 4-CL

Plate 26.

In Plate 26 the cat is interpreted as lying beside the fence, parallel with it, etc. These classifiers can also be used to show a change in the locative relationship between the cat and the fence through time. By tracing an arc with the bent-V classifier, starting on one side of the 4-classifier and passing over it to the other side, the signer communicates, 'The cat jumped over the fence.'

V̈-CL passes over 4-CL

Plate 27.

Now I will make explicit the difference between the SVO constructions and the locative constructions. Compare the relationship between the cat and the fence in the previous examples to the man and the fence in the following example. Suppose that for a fence a grammatical locus (L) has been established on the signer's right (e.g. L^r), and that a locus for a car has been established on the signer's left (L^l). This could be represented schematically in the following way.

(38)

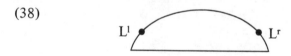

L^l L^r

If the signer subsequently directed the sign BUY toward the locus at the right established for a fence, this would indicate that the man bought the fence.

(39)   MAN BUY $[X:L^r]$

In other words, if a verb is directed toward a specific locus, the relationship specified by the verb will then hold between the subject of the verb and the referent associated with that locus. Since signers' movements, just like all movements performed by humans, are never exactly the same, and since the established locus is 'invisible', the signer will not always refer to the exact point on the arc which I have represented as L^r. That is, he might direct the verb BUY to the right of L^r or to the left of L^r. The amount of latitude possible undoubtedly depends on the number of loci established. I will represent this range of possible variation in the following way:

(40)

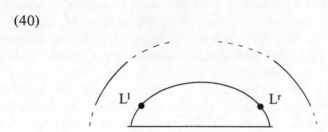

The solid line outside the original semicircle represents abstractly the points on the arc to which the signer could refer and still unambiguously indicate that a specific locus (L^r or L^l) was being referred to. However, if the signer does not point sufficiently close to the locus (represented by the dotted line or no line at all), then the signer is no longer making reference to that locus at all. That is, there would never be an interpretation such as, 'The man missed buying the fence by six inches', or, 'The man bought something six inches from the fence.' Rather, if the verb BUY is directed sufficiently close to the locus for the fence, then the man is interpreted as having bought the fence. What about the locus for a car established on the signer's left? If the form of the verb indicated that the man bought the fence, did he miss buying the car by several yards? Of course not. If the sign BUY is directed toward the fence locus, then the buying relationship specified by the verb will hold between the man and the fence — not between the man and the car. If the man bought the fence, then nothing at all is said about the man and the car.

The same is true for a verb like SEE. That is, it is either interpreted as having the referent associated with a specific locus as its object, or else there is no relationship at all. If the verb SEE is directed slightly to the side of a given locus, this is not interpreted to mean that the 'seeing' was done slightly to the side of the object. There is not a form of the verb meaning that the object was almost seen, as in, 'I only missed seeing it by a few inches.'

Notice that this is not true in the case of the locative predicates we have been examining in this section. In each instance there was a relationship between the fence and the cat, regardless of whether or not the bent-V classifier contacted or was directed toward the 4-classifier. The relationship between the two depended on the orientation of the individual classifiers, the location of the individual classifiers, and the (lack of) movement of the individual classifiers — but there was always a physical-locative relationship between the two classifiers.

It should be clear that there is a difference in the kind of relationships that are holding in these two types of constructions. When the classifiers are used, the spatial relationships between the classifiers signify spatial relationships between the objects represented by the classifiers. Changes in the spatial relationship between the two through time can also be shown ('The cat jumped over the fence.').

A verb like BUY, on the other hand, will have a subject and an object. The subject and object, as we have seen, will be indicated by word order and/or reference to grammatically established loci ('or', in the case of SOV order). If the appropriate conditions are met, correct word order and/or reference to a grammatical locus, then a specific relationship will be interpreted as holding between the subject and the object of that verb.

It should be clear that this is not true when the classifiers are present. In this case there is *always* a spatial relationship holding between the two classifiers, whether the classifiers are moving or not. In addition, the movement of a classifier does not have the same function as the movement of a verb like BUY or SEE which, if it changes form to indicate its object, does so by being directed or oriented toward the grammatical locus of that object. (This class of verbs has been called multidirectional [Friedman 1976].) The movement of a classifier indicates *movement* of what the classifier represents and may or may not be directed toward the other classifier. As a result of this difference, complex predicates involving two classifiers are not equivalent to a transitive verb. However, in spite of the fact that the classifiers show a spatial relationship between two entities, the two classifiers do not have the same significance. The first serves as a reference point, from which the location of some other entity (moving or stationary) can be identified. Taken as a figure–ground relationship, the reference entity would be the 'ground' and the stationary or active entity would be the 'figure'.

When these locative constructions are questioned, the locative object is not signed with the nonmanual question signal. For example, to ask if the cat is lying next to the fence, the signer would sign

$$\overline{\text{(41)} \quad \text{FENCE} \quad 4\text{-CL} \underline{\hspace{2cm}}^{q}}$$
$$\text{CAT } \ddot{\text{V}}\text{-CL} \quad (\ddot{\text{V}}\text{-CL is placed next to 4-CL})$$

where FENCE is not accompanied by the signal 'q', and where 4-CL is initially not accompanied by 'q'. The signal 'q' begins with the sign CAT. This is behaving like the earlier examples of topicalized objects with respect to the location of the 'q' signal, but differs in that the nonmanual signal 't' is not required.

As a result of these differences, I will not treat FENCE in the construction

(42)   FENCE   4-CL ⸺⸺⸺⸺
    CAT V̈-CL (V̈-CL is palm down, on top
            of, and parallel to 4-CL)
  'The cat is lying on the fence.'

as having the same relationship to V̈-CL that FENCE would have with a multidirectional verb like BUY. Rather, in (42) FENCE is the locative reference point from which we can know the location of the cat in the complex predicate consisting of the two classifiers and their relationship to one another.

Our reason for examining these sentences was that they had a word order which appeared to be object–subject–verb, with no required topic marking on the initial sign. We have argued, however, that the initial noun is not related to the locative predicate in the same way that it would be related to a multidirectional verb. Rather, it should be regarded as the locative reference point used in the complex predicate consisting of the two classifiers.

I will tentatively adopt the following terminology. Since FENCE in (42) is acted upon, functions as a 'ground' in a figure–ground relationship, and is less prominent than CAT (the 'figure' and more prominent member of the pair of signs), I will call FENCE in (42) the 'locative object', and CAT the 'locative subject'.

We can now distinguish two very distinct types of constructions:

Subject–Verb–Object (unmarked order with a transitive verb).

Locative Object–Locative Subject–Locative Predicate (unmarked order with a locative predicate).

There is clear evidence that these locative constructions can be complex (i.e. having a clause embedded within them).

(43)   FENCE (4-CL————————)

                            CAT SLEEP V̈-CL (V̈-CL is palm down, on

                                              top of, and parallel to

                                              4-CL)

        'A sleeping cat is lying on the fence.'

(The 4-classifier may not be present in the middle of this string in this case because of the possibility of using both hands to make the sign SLEEP.) Notice that right in the middle of this construction we find the clause, CAT SLEEP. In this example V̈–CL represents not just a cat, but a cat which is sleeping. One would never want to argue that FENCE CAT SLEEP formed any kind of a unit. Rather, the units appear to be FENCE, CAT SLEEP, and the locative predicate (i.e. we still see the order Locative Object–Locative Subject–Locative Predicate).

3.9. VERBS AND CLASSIFIERS

In the previous section we examined (briefly) the relationships between classifiers and word order. There it was pointed out that pairs of classifiers are signed in a way which reflects the spatial relationships of their denotata. It was shown that a noun used as a reference point is signed first, followed by the placement of a classifier for that object. The thing to be located is signed next. The relationship between the two is then shown in a spatial way by the location, movement, and orientation of the combination of classifiers.

In this section we will look at what happens to word order when lexical verbs and classifiers are used simultaneously. The following roughly corresponds to the English sentence, 'The man painted the bottom of the table':

(44)   TABLE B-CL $\underline{\text{(palm down)}}$

MAN PAINT [underside of B-CL]

Notice that here we do have a subject, a verb, and an object. The object is in initial position, yet it is not marked as the topic of the sentence. Also notice that the sign PAINT is not made against the flat palm facing the signer as it would be in citation form, but is made *underneath* the classifier representing the table. This is how the signer conveys the information that the man painted the underside of the table. This use of the sign PAINT is very specific in its meaning. The verb indicates not only what its object is, but which part of that object is being affected. Once again, the classifier is used to show the location of some action. The location of the verb sign with respect to the classifier indicates the location of the painting with respect to the table. It would seem reasonable to view TABLE in the example above as the locative object of the verb PAINT.

Further support for this conclusion comes from how questions are formed with this construction. Once again, we find that this construction behaves like the 'pure' locative construction in that the sign TABLE and the B-CL are not accompanied by the 'q' signal. The 'q' signal does not begin until the (locative?) subject is signed.

We have examined two very distinct types of constructions: subject–verb–object constructions, and locative constructions which use two classifiers and the spatial relationships between the classifiers to represent the spatial relationships between their denotata. We have also examined a third construction which combines elements of both. It uses a lexical verb, but uses the location and orientation of the verb to indicate the location and orientation of the action with respect to the object. We found that this 'mixed' construction behaved like the 'pure' locative construction with respect to word order and question formation.

We will next examine two other constructions which also behave like the locative constructions in these respects.

3.10. PANTOMIME

Signers can also show the relationship between an object and a person through the use of pantomimic behavior. That is, to show that a man reached into his pocket, pulled out a penny, and then dropped it over his shoulder, a signer could say PENNY MAN and then reach into his pocket, pull his hand out of his pocket with the thumb and index finger together as if holding a penny, move his hand to a position behind his shoulder, and then release the contact between the thumb and the index finger. In doing so the signer would have used only two lexical signs: PENNY and MAN. Everything else that followed was pantomimic. My description of the pantomimic activity is incomplete and abbreviated because naturally the movement of the head and eyes, the posture of the body, etc., also count as part of the pantomimic activity. The point of the example is that the signer did use two signs and in a given order. He first mentioned an object which was to be manipulated, and then mentioned the agent, whose gestures the signer's gestures would represent, and then he proceeded with the pantomimic activity. Of the two possible orders of PENNY and MAN, the order shown above is preferred by far among the signers I have consulted.

Unfortunately, this type of pantomimic behavior is not felicitously accompanied by the 'q' signal. Instead, the signers I have consulted tell me that after the pantomime is complete, they would use a manual question marker accompanied by the 'q' signal to ask if the preceding pantomime was accurate. As a result it is not possible to make a comparison with the other locative-type constructions in this respect. However, with respect to word order, the pantomimic sequences appear parallel to the locative constructions.

3.11. INFLECTED VERBS

Fischer and Gough (1974) examine ways that the form of ASL verbs can be changed to reflect either continuous or habitual aspect. Later research by Carlene Pedersen and Ursula Bellugi, in particular, Klima and Bellugi (1979: 243–271), investigates several other changes in the motion of the verb which also reflect aspect. I will not go into the details of either of these investigations, but merely note that the presence of such inflected verb forms seems to have an effect on the word order that is preferred. Pedersen (personal communication) feels that if the inflected verb form is used, the sentence is most naturally signed with the object of the verb in initial position.[9]

An important question with respect to these constructions is whether or not the initial objects in these constructions are topics. They can appear in initial position without any topic marking (including no lengthening of the duration of the sign). This suggests that in addition to topicalization, which can change the underlying word order, this type of inflected verb also has an effect on the word order. It is interesting to note that with respect to grammatical processes like question formation, these preposed objects behave as the 'locative objects' did. That is, to ask if the girl ate tomatoes for a long time, the initial sign TOMATO would not be signed as part of the question.

$$\overline{\qquad\qquad\qquad}^{q}$$

(45)   TOMATO GIRL EAT[I:durative aspect]
     'Did the girl eat tomatoes for a long time?'

We can conclude from this that in addition to topicalization, certain types of verb inflection also have an effect on the surface word order. Namely, the object is moved to initial position and is structurally separate from the main clause. We can represent this in the same way that we represented the topicalized objects:

(46)

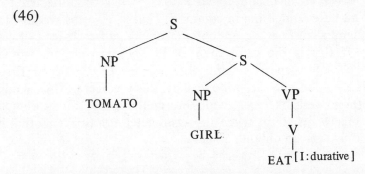

The reason for this may be due to the heaviness of the verb. The verb is not only inflected for durative aspect but, because of the inflection, the verb also takes longer to sign.

Ross (1967) discusses a rule of Complex NP Shift for English, which has the effect of placing a 'heavy' noun phrase at the end of a clause. Consider the following two sentences, from Ross (1967):

(47)   He attributed the fire to a short circuit.
(48)   *He attributed to a short circuit the fire.

This pair of sentences demonstrates that the normal position for the direct object in English is directly after the verb. The second sentence is unacceptable because the direct object, 'the fire', is not directly after the verb.

Notice, however, that if the direct object is 'heavy', it can be moved to final position in the clause.

(49)   He attributed the fire which destroyed most of my factory to a short circuit.
(50)   He attributed to a short circuit the fire which destroyed most of my factory.

The effect of this rule is to make sure that the 'heavy' constituent is in clause-final position in surface structure. Notice that this is exactly what is accomplished in the ASL sentences with the 'heavy' verb when the object is moved to initial position. The verb ends up in final position not through being moved there but because the object was moved to initial position.

Alternatively, it could be possible that 'locative constructions', mixed constructions with a lexical verb and a classifier, pantomimic constructions, and constructions with verbs inflected for aspect all have something in common. That is, it seems possible to view them all as having an oblique object rather than a direct object. If this is the case, then all of the constructions would follow a single generalization: oblique objects are signed first, followed by the subject, followed by the predicate. This would mean that a verb like EAT, which normally takes a direct object, would change its status when it was inflected for aspect, so that it would only take an oblique object.

3.12.   SUMMARY

We have seen that word order in ASL is anything but random. The basic word order in ASL is subject–verb–object. This underlying structure can be changed by topicalizing the subject, the object, or the verb phrase. This is true for both multidirectional verbs and nonmultidirectional verbs.

SVO   Underlying structure.

S,VO Topicalized subject.

O,SV Topicalized object.

VO,S Topicalized verb phrase.

We also found that if the signing space was used in a significant way, subject–object–verb order was also possible.

ASL also has other ways of expressing the relationship between two things. ASL can use classifiers to show a locative relationship between two entities or between an object and an action. If classifiers are used, then there is also a regular order. To show a locative relationship between two entities, a reference point is established by the first entity, the thing to be located is signed next, and then classifiers for both entities are presented simultaneously in a way that directly reflects the actual physical relationship of the sign denotata. Similarly, if a classifier is used to show the relationship between an object and an action, the object is signed first, the agent is signed second, and then the object and the action are represented simultaneously by either two classifiers or a classifier and a verb.

We can see evidence for two major types of constructions: subject–verb–object constructions and constructions with oblique objects. Included in this oblique category are 'locative objects', 'pantomimic objects', and objects of verbs inflected for aspect. In all these oblique constructions the object is mentioned first, followed by the subject, followed by the predicate (or pantomime).

Historical evidence suggests that one hundred years ago this was not the case. In the next section we will summarize Fischer's analysis of ASL one hundred years ago and her analysis of the processes which resulted in the change.

3.13. FISCHER ON WORD-ORDER CHANGE

Fischer (1975) argues that in the 1870s, the sign language used at that time, which was presumably the ancestor of present-day ASL, had an unmarked subject–object–verb order instead of the subject–verb–object order which she claims is underlying in present-day ASL. Evidence for this subject–object–verb order is found in the *American Annals of the Deaf*, generally in regard to a debate between educators of the deaf at that time as to the natural order of thought. One side held that English exemplified the natural order of thought and that the 'colloquial order', what the deaf did in spite of the efforts of educators to change their language, involved reversing the natural order of thought. The first reference I have seen on this subject goes back to 1859 in an article written by J. A. Jacobs in what was then called *The American Annals of the Deaf and Dumb*. The following two citations from that article illustrate his thinking:

Let me premise, that I mean by signs, significant gesticulations only, the vehicle of ideas to deaf-mutes; whether I use them in the colloquial order of the mute, or as the means of interpreting written language, following the order of the words (1859: 66).

I wish to teach a beginner the combination of the adjective and noun — 'A black dog'. Colloquially I teach and illustrate the words separately. I then combine them. He is now almost prepared to connect the two words together in thought — the quality and its substantive. Now if in attempting to point out and form this connection in his mind, I should do it by colloquial signs, I reverse the order of the thought and words, and communicate to him the connection in the order of 'A dog black' (1859: 69).

Twelve years later the Rev. J. R. Keep argues in what had by then come to be called *The American Annals of the Deaf*, that the sign language, and not English, follows the natural order of thought.

. . . the placing of the object before the action, is, it will be seen, a striking feature of the sign-language. That in this respect it follows the method in which all minds conceive of objects and actions, we have no doubt. Take this as an illustration, and, as it seems to us, proof of the point. Suppose I strike a board. I do not strike vacant air, seeing nothing, and having no idea of anything before me until after I have struck, when suddenly a board rises up to receive the blow. I first *see* the board, I intend to strike it, and with it before my sight, I strike. In exact conformity with this necessary order of nature and of fact, in describing this in signs we say, 'I a board strike' (1871a: 224).

I will not be taking a stand here on the natural order of thought, but will merely note that both men agreed that the sign language used by the deaf at that time had a word order which differed from English and placed the object before the verb. Fischer argues that both direct and indirect evidence indicate that the unmarked order used at that time was subject–object–verb, as in 'I a board strike.' Another example from Keep (1871a) illustrates an SOV construction which is not acceptable in present-day ASL.

(51)   SON YOUNGER MONEY ALL TAKE

Recall that Fischer also argues that now the unmarked order in ASL is subject–verb–object. Table 1 is a summary of Fischer's view as to how ASL, within the short time of one hundred years, changed from a subject–object–verb language to a subject–verb–object language.

Initially SOV was the unmarked order, though there is evidence that OSV order also occurred (Keep 1871a). Table 1 represents Fischer's account of the change from SOV to SVO as the unmarked order in ASL.

Table 1. *Fischer's analysis of the change from SOV to SVO*

Stage	SOV	SVO	OSV
1 (1871)	Unmarked	—	Marked
2	Marked – locational verbs	—	Unmarked – locational verbs
3	Marked – all verbs	—	Unmarked – all verbs
4	Marked – all verbs	Marked – topicalized subject (borrowed from English)	Unmarked – all verbs
5 (1975)	Marked – all verbs	Unmarked	Marked – topicalized object

The change from Stage 1 to Stage 2 was motivated, according to Fischer, by the economy of motion used in signing OSV order with directional verbs. That is, some verbs can indicate the grammatical relations of subject and object by their direction of movement or orientation (Fischer 1975; Lacy 1974; Friedman 1976; and others). Fischer illustrates this with some possible ways of signing 'The girl kicked the boy' in ASL. One possible way to do so in ASL would be to simply sign GIRL KICK BOY. Fischer claims that in a more extended discourse, the most natural way to sign the meaning of 'the girl kicked the boy' is by establishing locations for the girl and the boy and indicating who kicked whom by the direction of the verb KICK (1975: 19). The location of BOY is established first, the location of GIRL next, and then the verb KICK moves from the location of GIRL to the location of BOY. Thus, if BOY is established on the right and GIRL is established on the left, then the entire sentence is accomplished with three movements: (1) the object is established on the right, (2) the subject is established on the left, and (3) the verb (which is already on the left) moves from left to right. Compare this with the less economical subject–object–verb order: (1) the subject is established on the left, (2) the object is established on the right, (3) the hands move back to the left, and (4) the verb then moves from left to right. The subject–object–verb order in this example requires an extra, and meaningless, transitional movement: the transition from the location of the object back to the location of the subject so that the verb can be signed. This is the motivation which Fischer claimed was responsible for the change from Stage 1 to Stage 2. Fischer argues that the change from Stage 2 to Stage 3 was simply a generalization of the use of the unmarked OSV order from use with locational verbs to use with all verbs. In Stage 4 the influence of English is felt and the SVO order is used when the signer wants to topicalize the subject. Thus, in Stage 4 SVO order is still a marked order and OSV is unmarked. The last stage is present-day ASL.

There are a number of problems with this analysis, including the fact that there is no evidence for any of the stages between the first and the last. I find the analysis unnecessarily complicated because of this lack of evidence for these intermediate stages. In addition, Fischer does not include in her analysis some of the present-day word-order restrictions we have been discussing.

3.14. REANALYSIS OF THE HISTORICAL CHANGE FROM SOV TO SVO

The texts which are available indicate that subject–object–verb order was definitely unmarked in ASL in the 1870s. Fischer is very clear about this. She also presents an isolated example of a sentence using subject–verb–object order and a sentence using object–subject–verb order. Since the example of the object–subject–verb order will turn out to be important for the discussion which follows, I will quote the entire passage in which it is presented:

Suppose that the deaf-mute at the very beginning of his efforts to learn language, has come to know the words *cat*, and *catch*, and *boy*. Making the sign for cat, which we do by putting the thumb and forefinger of each hand to the mouth as if taking hold of whiskers, and then stroking the back of the left hand to indicate the fur; then locating the animal; then, having made the sign for boy, we represent him as catching the cat, and write for the child the sentence, 'A boy catches a cat.' Does he now know what it means, and is there any difficulty in his modeling other sentences after this form? None whatever (Keep 1871a).

The wording used in the passage seems to indicate that the action of catching the cat may have been represented by panto-mimic behavior rather than a lexical verb. Keep originally says that he is talking about three words: *cat, catch*, and *boy*. When he is talking about *cat* and *boy*, he talks about *making the sign* in both cases. However, he then changes his terminology and says, 'we represent him as catching the cat'. If it is pantomimic, then it is no different from what is possible today (cf. section 3.11). In modern ASL, assuming that a signer presented a pantomime of a boy catching a cat, the same signs would be made in the same order. The only difference would be in the obvious difference in the actual form of the sign CAT then and now. It is clear that signers then, as now, did use pantomime to one degree or another. In another 1871 article (Keep 1871b), the use of pantomime is shown in much greater detail:

By a few movements of the arms, the bear is placed before you – then, the man appears, gun in hand – he sees the bear – the gun comes down from the shoulder in deliberate and careful aim – it is fired – the bear falls dead upon the ground. The end sought is to give, so far as possible, an exact reproduction of the scene, and it is attained to a degree far beyond what the most elaborate and skillful painting could effect. Not only are the objects brought in vivid distinctness before the mind, but the actions performed, instead of being left to inference and suggestion, as they must be in a painting, actually take place before our eyes (Keep 1871b: 18).

The paragraph above does not mention the word 'pantomime', but there are suggestions of pantomime being used: 'The end sought is to give . . . an exact reproduction of the scene', and 'the actions performed . . . actually take place before our eyes.'

In addition, in present-day ASL there are no lexical signs for 'bringing a gun down from the shoulder', or 'deliberate and careful aim'. Both these events would be represented pantomimically. The signer would recreate (to some degree) the actual movements that he wished to communicate.

Now let us take one last look at the example of the boy catching the cat. Keep says that the signer represents the boy as catching the cat, rather than saying that we next make the sign CATCH. If Keep had been describing present-day ASL he could make exactly the same statement. The signer today would represent the boy as 'catching' the cat rather than making the sign CATCH. While there is no set way to represent the boy as 'catching' the cat, the signers I have consulted used both hands as if they were actually picking up a cat around its middle. Though ASL has a sign CATCH, it is not appropriate to use it in this context. The sign CATCH could be used if the boy had been chasing the cat; but with the cat located in a specific area, the signers I have consulted feel that to use the sign CATCH is very strange. In the case of a stationary cat it is more appropriate to pick it up than to 'catch' it.

Because of this strong possibility that the example of OSV order contained pantomime rather than a lexical sign, I see no reason to posit a marked object–subject–verb order used in 1871, as Fischer (1975) does. Rather, I will assume that the sign language of 1871 had not only a word order which expressed grammatical relationships (subject–object–verb), but also more pantomimic ways of representing the relationship between two (or more) things. If a pantomimic representation is used (then and now), the object to be related to the actor represented in the pantomime is named first, the actor is named second, and the pantomime is third. In other words, if the assumption above is correct, there is absolutely no difference between the sequence described by the Rev. Keep and the sequence which is made now more than one hundred years later (except for the difference in the form of the sign CAT).

Before trying to account for the change in word order from SOV to SVO in the last century, it will be helpful to make a comparison of the word orders used in both stages.

1871   SOV order was unmarked (multidirectional verbs and nonmultidirectional verbs).

Pantomimic sequences named first the object, then the actor, and then proceeded with the pantomime.

Classifiers?

1977   SVO order is unmarked for multidirectional verbs and nonmultidirectional verbs. (The subject, object, or verb phrase can be topicalized.)

Pantomimic seqences name first the object, then the actor, and then proceed with the pantomime.

Sequences with classifiers name first the reference point, then the object or action to be located, then the verb.

SOV order can be used if the relationships are shown spatially.

Our knowledge of the sign language used in 1871 is obviously incomplete, based on small bits of data, etc., but there is one obvious difference between the sign language of 1871 and the sign language of today: in 1871 SOV order was unmarked, while today SVO order is unmarked. The analysis I would like to present seems to me to be very simple and straightforward.

By comparing the two sets of word-order characteristics, it can be seen that in 1871 there was evidence for the oblique construction in pantomimic sequences — no different from what is currently used. The only difference which is clear between then and now is that the unmarked order then was apparently SOV while now it is SVO. It does not appear necessary to postulate the existence of three separate stages between then and now. In particular, there is no evidence for the claim that OSV was ever an unmarked order for locational verbs (i.e. not involving topicalization), and later an unmarked order for all verbs, still later to become a marked order (i.e. involving topicalization).

I would like to suggest, just as Fischer suggested, that during the past century SVO order, because of the obvious influence of English, has replaced SOV order as the unmarked order. SOV order has become marked and now can only be used if the relationship between the subject and the object is shown spatially. In addition, a rule of topicalization, if there wasn't one already, has been incorporated into the language.

NOTES

1. Recall from 2.3.1.4 that DOG in this construction would be accompanied by the head nod 'hn'.
2. A large number of verbs in ASL change their movement or orientation to indicate agent/experiencer/source and patient/beneficiary/goal; the sign moves away from the location, real or grammatically established, of the former and toward the latter (Friedman 1976). A very small number of exceptions appear to work in the opposite way. Fischer's claim appears to be that if such 'multi-directional' verbs are used, the SOV order is possible.
3. Some explanation is needed here regarding the notation used in (12). The notation indicates a lack of continuity in the question signal which accompanies FORGET PURSE and the question signal which accompanies the sign WOMAN. There may be, in fact, no such break in the continuity of the signal. What actually could happen is this: the first question is asked normally, which includes a lengthening in the duration of the final sign in the sentence (cf. Friedman and Battison 1973; Friedman 1976). The second question is signed as if the end of the first question constituted both a neutral facial expression and a neutral body position. By assuming that the end of the previous question constituted 'neutrality', it is necessary, in order to ask another question, to move the head (and body) further forward and to further raise the eyebrows. This is exactly what could happen in ·the two-question sequence shown.
4. A videotape machine records 60 fields per second. It is possible to replay a videotape field by field so that what is happening every sixtieth of a second can be observed.
5. Friedman (1976) makes a distinction between 'nominal intonation' and 'question intonation'. Apparently 'nominal intonation' is the way a given sign is made if it is neither a topic nor part of a question. As was seen in Chapter 2, there are many possible facial expressions which are completely unrelated to either questioning or topicalization. We will be making a distinction between topic marking and question marking, both of which Friedman calls 'question intonation'. However, the reason for bringing this up here is that Friedman also notes a difference in timing between 'nominal intonation' and 'question intonation' accompanying a single sign. She claims that 'question intonation' involves raising the eyebrows, furrowing the brows, and holding the questioned sign for an extra beat. In other words, Friedman also notes that certain signs are held longer than they would otherwise be held, and accompanied by a brow raise (though she does not mention head position).
6. The notation '([X: pro.1]' indicates the motion of this multidirectional verb. In this case it was directed toward the signer. I have used lower case letters (pro.1) because I do not mean to imply that the pronoun PRO.1 is part of the verb — only that the verb makes reference to the same person that PRO.1 makes reference to (i.e. the signer).
7. Actually, one of my informants finds both ways of producing the string equally unacceptable.
8. Many examples of this type are discussed in DeMatteo (1977). He argues that in

examples like these it makes no sense to use terms like grammatical subject and object. Instead, he argues that these classifier constructions are the surface realization of a visual–spatial underlying representation rather than a semantic representation consisting of semantic primitives.

9. Apparently there is some variability in whether signers do, in fact, place the object in initial position, since Bellugi (personal communication) has noticed objects following such inflected verb forms in everyday conversation.

4

Subordination

4.0. INTRODUCTION

The notion of subordination has been both implicit and explicit in previous work on ASL, including Stokoe et al. (1965), Fischer (1973, 1975), and others. This is not surprising since subordination is a phenomenon which has been assumed to be a part of all natural languages.

One can talk about subordination at an underlying level or at the level of surface structure. One can talk about subordination at the semantic level of representation, whether or not this is reflected in the surface structure as subordination. For example, Langacker and Munro (1975) claim that all sentences in English which characterize a process rather than a state have the existential predicate DO_p in their semantic representations, such that the clause structure which is subordinate to it structurally is within its scope. Thus the English sentence 'Martin lives' would have as part of its semantic representation that shown in (1) on the next page. Langacker points out that the predicate DO_p is not necessarily realized on the surface. That is, the structure above is part of the semantic representation of the sentence 'Martin lives', which is not a complex sentence and does not contain a manifestation of the predicate DO_p on the surface.

Even when DO_p is realized on the surface, it does not change a simple sentence to a complex sentence (i.e. the sentence 'Martin does not still live here' is not complex). On the other hand, subordination can be used to describe facts about surface structure. In this usage we will mean that in surface structure one clause is

(1)

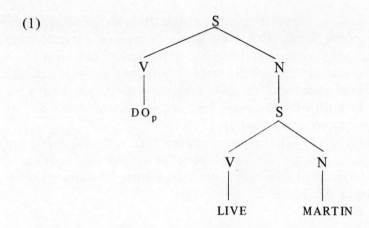

part of another clause; that the two are not joined coordinately. This type of surface-structure embedding is exemplified by the following English sentences:

(2) I figured out that *John had gone*.
(3) The man *who wore the flower* likes your sister.

In (2) a single sentence is made up of two clausal parts: 'I figured out' and 'John had gone'. 'I figured out' is incomplete as a simple sentence; it requires the specification of its object. Its object, in this case, is a clause which is marked as a noun phrase by the subordinating conjunction 'that'. These structural relationships can be shown in the following way:

(4)

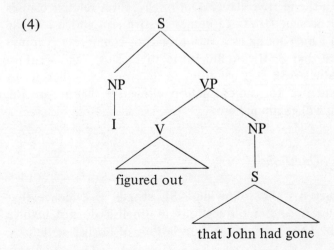

The conjunction 'that' and the clause 'John had gone' together, form a noun phrase. This noun phrase is part of a larger clause structure and functions as the object of the verb 'figured out'.

In the second sentence illustrated above, one clause is actually nested within another: 'The man *who wore the flower* likes your sister.' In both of these cases we have absolutely clear cases of surface-structure subordination.

Thompson (1977) tentatively claims that ASL does not have any surface structures which involve subordination. Because of the importance of this claim, we will examine Thompson's arguments in detail.

4.1. ARGUMENTS AGAINST SUBORDINATION

Thompson (1977) was led to suspect that there was no subordination in ASL by his failure to find evidence for the existence of relative clauses in ASL. His informant was provided with English sentences containing relative clauses and produced ASL translations of those sentences. Thompson transcribed the signs that were produced and the order that they were produced in. Some of the data also includes the location of pauses. Based on this data, Thompson was unable to find evidence for the existence of relative clauses. As we shall see in Chapter 5, however, the marker for restrictive relative clauses in ASL is not produced by the hands, but is a special facial expression and head position which is co-extensive with the relative clause. Optionally, these relative clauses also contain the sign THATa (a demonstrative sign which is made with no base hand) acting as a subordinator. At any rate, Thompson concluded that ASL contains no relative clauses and went on to examine other ASL constructions to determine whether or not there was evidence for subordination elsewhere. Those are the arguments we will examine here.

4.1.1. Indirect Questions

Thompson presents the following ASL strings as evidence that ASL analogues of indirect questions in English do not involve subordination. The first two are translations of English sentences.

The numbers following some of the examples below indicate the numbering in Thompson (1977). The transcription used in Thompson (1977) has been adapted to make it consistent with that used here.

(5) 'He was still angry so he refused to tell me whether or not they had called.'

ANGRY NOT TELL[X: pro.1] FINISH CALL O-R NOT-YET CALL (19)

(6) 'The child must do whatever the mother says.'
CHILD MUST FOLLOW MOTHER TELL CHILD (20)

Thompson claims that the two ASL strings are polysentential paraphrases of the English because there are sentence breaks (pauses) 'presumably occurring after ANGRY and TELL[X: pro.1] in (19) [(5)] and after FOLLOW in (20) [(6)]' (1977: 189). Thompson argues that pauses greater than 0.4 to 0.5 seconds are interpretable almost exclusively as sentence boundaries or as performance difficulties. Since his argument for the presence of sentence boundaries depends on the presence of such pauses, he has made no argument for the examples above because of the 'presumably'.

The third sentence presented as evidence that ASL analogues of indirect questions in English lack subordination was produced first in ASL and translated into English (apparently by Thompson).

(7) $\overline{}$PRO.1$^+$ ASK $\overline{\text{PRO.1 BORROW BOOK}}^{\text{q}}$ (21)
'I asked if I could borrow the book.'

The '+' is used by Thompson to indicate the presence of eye contact, and the '−' to indicate the lack of eye contact. Thompson indicates that the string PRO.1 BORROW BOOK is signed as a question. I would like to suggest that, just as Thompson claims, that is an example of direct speech. As a result, I am at a loss as to why he translated it as indirect speech. A more proper translation would seem to be, 'I asked him, "Can I borrow the book?".' If this is correct, then the example presented is not an example of an ASL analogue of indirect questions in English at all, and should not be used as evidence concerning ASL analogues of indirect questions. Thompson makes the same claims about the other two examples he presents as analogues of indirect questions, so I will not discuss them separately here.

I do not fully understand his next argument. He states that several examples involving the verbs KNOW and NOT-KNOW are resistant to being analyzed as some form of direct speech. He states that several instances of KNOW HOW . . . and KNOW WHY . . . were observed, but there was some indication that the pairs of signs formed a compound verb. Unfortunately he does not state what that evidence is, or what the significance of such compounds would be.

Unfortunately, he does not provide complete sentences involving KNOW HOW . . . or KNOW WHY. . . , so that the pause data and accompanying nonmanual signals could be demonstrated in these cases as well. These cases would seem to be important to examine closely since potential markers of subordination are present in the surface structure.

I have seen no evidence for calling any occurrences of either KNOW WHY or KNOW HOW compound verbs except for the fact that long pauses do not occur between the signs. However, KNOW does appear to have formed a compound with THAT. This sign is often confused with the sign DON'T-KNOW by people learning ASL. This is because the motion and handshape of the compound KNOW THAT can be exactly the same as that for BAD (a historically merged form of GOOD and negation). The sign KNOW THAT is made higher than chin level which keeps it distinct from the sign BAD. This compound sign will not take a simple direct object, as is shown by the following ungrammatical string.

(8)   * PRO.1 KNOW THAT GIRL

The compound either occurs with no overt complement:

(9)   PRO.1 KNOW THAT
       'I already know that.'
       (Note the special meaning associated with this compound.)

or it takes a sentential complement:

(10)   PRO.1 KNOW͡ THAT GIRL TALL
      'I already know that the girl is tall.'

When it is followed by a clause, as in the example above, there is no pause between the compound verb and what follows. This seems to be strong evidence in favor of a subordination analysis of this structure.

In addition to the sentence types presented by Thompson in which real question forms follow verbs like SAY and KNOW (illustrated below),

(11) $^-$PRO.1$^+$ ASK$^-$ $\overline{\text{PRO.1 BORROW BOOK}}^{\text{q}}$ (21)[1]
      'I asked, "Can I borrow the book?".'

(12)   MARK WANT KNOW/WHAT ASA GIVE HENRY WHAT[2] (23)
      'Mark wanted to know. What did Asa give Henry?'

I have also seen, in both elicited sentences and stories, constructions in which the second clause is not signed as a question.

(13)   DON'T-KNOW WHERE GONE
      'He didn't know where he had gone.'

Sentence (13) is from the telling of 'The Sorcerer's Apprentice' where Fritzl has been magically transported from one place to another. In this case there is no indication of WHERE GONE being in the form of a question and no pause anywhere in the string. I see no reason to analyze this construction in the same way I would analyze the constructions which Thompson illustrates. They are obviously different. The example presented above, in contrast to the examples presented by Thompson, seems to be a perfect candidate for a subordinate-clause analysis.

4.1.2. Direct versus indirect speech

In the next part of his paper Thompson attempts to argue that ASL does not distinguish between direct and indirect speech. He points out that there is a straightforward difference in English between direct and indirect speech.

(14)   John said that he saw Bill. (indirect)
(15)   John said, 'I saw Bill.' (direct)

He then illustrates that ASL does not distinguish between these two by presenting examples like the following with the verb TELL:

(16)   PRO.1 TELL $^+$ FRIEND $^-$ PRO.1 DOUBT GO (24)
       'I told my friend that I doubted I would go.'

It is not at all clear whether this is direct or indirect speech. Our only evidence that this is indirect speech is the translation that Thompson provides. We saw earlier, however, that even examples which were argued by him to be direct speech were translated by him as indirect speech.

He claims that the following facts about ASL support his claim that ASL does not distinguish between direct and indirect speech:

Support for this idea comes from the following additional facts: the narration of reported speech or thought is often accompanied by a slight change in body orientation, indicating adoption of the role of the reported speaker; first person pronouns often replace third person ones; and the verb of saying or thinking sometimes occurs both at the beginning and end, like quotation marks, delimiting the reported speech from the speaker's own (Thompson 1977: 190).

Thompson's argument would strongly support his contention if speakers always changed their body orientation to indicate adoption of the role of the reported speaker and, as a result, always changed their pronominal reference. However, this is not what he reports. He reports that it happens often. One could well ask what the signer does when he does not adopt the role of the reported speaker and doesn't change his pronominal reference. In fact, Thompson's observations about ASL support the idea that ASL does distinguish between direct and indirect speech. That is, ASL also makes a straightforward distinction between direct and indirect speech.

In direct speech the signer changes the orientation of his body (as Thompson reports), and he also changes his pronominal reference so that first-person reference no longer refers to the signer, but to the reported speaker. In fact, when this is done, the verb

SAY is not even required. The following example illustrates this type of construction:

(17) JOHN (SAY)^{shift}PRO.1 TIRED
'John said, "I'm tired." '

The same event could be reported as follows:

(18) JOHN SAY PRO.3 TIRED
'John$_i$ said he$_i$ was tired.'

This is exactly the distinction which Thompson claims does not exist. In fact, this is exactly the distinction which the facts he presents support (i.e. sometimes signers change their pronominal reference and sometimes they do not). My own observations about these two types of constructions are that the 'direct speech' constructions seem to be present more often in narratives where role playing in general occurs often. That is, the choice between direct speech and indirect speech is a matter of style rather than of possibility.

4.1.3. Extension to other verbs

Feeling that he has established that ASL does not distinguish between direct and indirect speech but uses only direct speech, Thompson goes on to claim that other apparent verb–complement constructions are also analyzable as direct speech. In this category he includes verbs like SEE, FEEL, and THINK. In each case Thompson feels that 'the so-called main verb is merely a context establishing comment on the important part, the reported act, speech, or thought which follows' (1977: 190).

However, consider the evidence he presents:

(19) PRO.1 FEEL (20) HENRY GOOD WRITE PAPER (28)
'I expect Henry to write a good paper.'
(The ASL string is a translation of the English.)

The '(20)' between FEEL and HENRY indicates a pause of approximately one-third of a second. If Thompson is correct, that what follows the so-called main verb is a reported act, speech, or thought, then we would expect a shift in pronominal reference to occur in this type of example, just as it does in direct speech. However, Thompson's examples have first-person subjects with the main verb, so we would not expect any shift in pronominal reference in them. Suppose that instead of a first-person subject, example (19) had a third-person subject in the main clause and a first-person subject in the second clause:

> (20)   JOHN FEEL PRO.1 LUCKY
>   'John feels that I am lucky.'

Thompson would apparently predict that this should mean, 'John feels that he is lucky.' However, the PRO.1 in the above example refers to the speaker, not to John. This is not 'direct speech', or 'direct thought'. In fact, it is parallel to the previous examples of indirect speech.

Thompson next discusses the verbs HAPPY, ANGRY, SURPRISED, RELIEVED, SORRY, and PROMISE. He claims that these are not complement-taking verbs in ASL, and in general this is in accordance with my own observations of the use of these verbs.

He then takes up the verbs KNOW, DOUBT, and BELIEVE, and presents the following two examples:

> (21)   PRO.2 KNOW/MARK HATE CIGARETTE (33)
>   ('/' indicates a pause longer than a second.)
>
> (22)   LYNN KNOW FOR-SURE NOTHING HAPPEN (34)

He observes that there may or may not be any pauses after the verb KNOW, and suggests three possible analyses for this type of construction: (a) this is Signed English; (b) it should be analyzed as were THINK and FEEL (comment–report coordinate analysis); or (c) it involves subordination.

Thompson does not make any claims about which analysis he feels would be the most appropriate, but, based on his not having found evidence for subordination elsewhere in the language, he feels that the third is the least likely.

It is difficult to know, without having seen the data, how to analyze a sequence like (21). The ASL string PRO.2 KNOW/MARK HATE CIGARETTE was given to Thompson as a translation of the

English sentence, 'It is obvious that Mark hates cigarettes.' Signers tell me that one way of expressing that something is obvious (or should be known) is by signing PRO.2 KNOW with a look of irritation on the face. This seems to be quite similar to English expressions like 'You should know that' or 'You know what I mean.' Unfortunately, Thompson does not provide any data concerning the presence of nonmanual behaviors during this string.

In spite of the obvious differences, Thompson lumps this construction together with constructions like (22), where no pause occurs and where, based on the semantics of the lexical items, a subordination analysis is natural. His observation about the data is that, in this group, pauses sometimes occur. This is not surprising, considering the way he groups his data.

In fact, one could make the same argument about English. Notice that in English, pauses sometimes occur after the word 'that' and sometimes they do not:

a. You should know that the world is round.
b. You should know that! / The world is round!

The fact that pauses sometimes occur after 'that' does not allow us to conclude that 'that' is not acting as a subordinator in (a). Rather, we realize that these two examples are different and analyze them differently.

Informants I have consulted say that there is a difference between (21), where there is a long pause after KNOW, and the following sentence:

(23)   PRO.2 KNOW MARK HATE CIGARETTE (no pauses)
       'You know Mark hates cigarettes.'

I would like to suggest that, just as Thompson claims, a long pause (roughly half a second or longer) can be interpreted as a sentence boundary or performance difficulty. It follows from this that if a pause can follow a verb, as in (21),

(21)   PRO.2 KNOW/MARK HATE CIGARETTE
       'You know [what I mean]. Mark hates cigarettes.'

this may be a reflection on the fact that PRO.2 KNOW and MARK HATE CIGARETTE are separate sentences. In fact, this seems to be a very reasonable approach to take. It does not follow that the same string without the pause also consists of two separate sentences. In fact, the evidence we have seen seems to indicate that this is not the case.

If Thompson had looked at questions, he may not have made the claims that he did. Consider the following string: REMEMBER DOG CHASE CAT. This can be signed as a single question or as a pair of questions:

(24) $\overline{\text{REMEMBER DOG CHASE CAT}}^{\text{q}}$
'Do you remember that the dog chased the cat?'

(25) $\overline{\text{REMEMBER}}^{\text{q}} \; \overline{\text{DOG CHASE CAT}}^{\text{q}}$
'Do you remember? Did the dog chase the cat?'

(26) $\overline{\text{REMEMBER DOG}}^{\text{q}} \; \overline{\text{CHASE CAT}}^{\text{q}}$
'Do you remember the dog? Did he chase the cat?'

In the first example the nonmanual signal for the yes–no question remains essentially the same throughout, and the string is considered to be a single question. However, if the signer puts a break between REMEMBER and DOG (a temporal break and a break in the nonmanual signal), he is asking two questions. If he puts a break between DOG and CHASE, he is also asking two questions, but the questions are different. The point is that without any breaks, the signer is not asking two questions, but one.

Thompson next looks at the verbs WANT, STOP, and FORGET. He presents sentences like the following:

(27)   PRO.1 TODAY STOP WORK (36)
'. . . I'm quitting today.'

(28)   LYNN FORGET TELL CLASS (37)
'Lynn forgot to tell the class that . . . '

(29)   PRO.1 WANT PRO.3 TEACH[X: pro.1] VIDEO-TAPE (38)
'I wanted him to teach me to videotape.'

He notes that in his data, there are never any significant pauses between these verbs and the clauses which follow them. Based on his earlier observation about the significance of pauses in ASL, he might have taken this as a reflection that these structures involve not two separate sentences but a single complex sentence. Thompson does not adopt this approach. He suggests that this set of verbs might in fact be auxiliaries or modals. He notes, however, that modals do not allow different subjects, which would eliminate WANT from this analysis. He then leaves this problem and promises to return to it later. However, the article contains no further reference to the problems posed by these verbs.

4.2. TWO MORE ARGUMENTS

Before leaving the question of subordination, I will present two more types of data which are naturally accounted for in an analysis involving subordination, but which an analysis like Thompson's would be unable to account for. Consider the following sentence:

(30) $\overline{\quad\quad t\quad}$
GIRL JOHN WANT AVOID
'As for the girl, John wants to avoid her.'

If WANT and AVOID were coordinate, the meaning of the sentence above should be something like, 'As for the girl, John wants and avoids her.' This is not the meaning of the sentence. Semantically, it is clear that wanting and avoiding are not two things that John is doing.

Recall from 2.3.1.4 that a pronoun coreferential with the subject of a sentence can follow that sentence for emphasis. This is shown by the example below:

(31) $\overline{\quad\quad hn\quad}$
MAN BUY CAR PRO.3
'The man bought the car, he did.'

Earlier it was also claimed that in a negative sentence, the pronoun would be accompanied by a side-to-side headshake. In the following example this occurs but involves more than a single clause:

(32) $\overline{\quad\quad\quad\quad\quad\quad\quad\quad\quad\quad n\quad}$
PRO.1 NOT EXPECT PRO.2 COME PRO.1
'I didn't expect you to come, I didn't.'

If, in fact, the two clauses are separate, the final pronoun would have to be PRO.2, not PRO.1, because the subject of the final clause is PRO.2. The fact that PRO.1 can appear in this position suggests that this is a single complex clause with PRO.1 as the subject of the main clause. Secondly, if the two clauses above were coordinate, or independent, why does the side-to-side headshake accompany the nonnegative PRO.2 COME?

4.3. SUMMARY

To sum up, Thompson has in no way made a case for the lack of subordination in ASL, even based on the data which he provides. His claim that ASL does not distinguish between direct and indirect speech (that ASL uses only direct speech) was not supportable. In fact, the evidence he presented argued against that claim. His attempt to extend this analysis to other types of verbs, such as SEE and FEEL, did not work because these verbs do not seem to be followed by any 'direct speech'. Instead, pronominal reference continued to be from the point of view of the speaker. Finally, he does not even propose an analysis of the verbs KNOW, STOP, FORGET, and WANT, which were never followed by pauses in his data.

In the next chapter we will examine a major form of subordination in ASL — restrictive relative clauses.

NOTES

1. Thompson's notation indicates that PRO.1 BORROW is accompanied by what he calls 'question intonation' with the brows furrowed and the eyebrows raised, but that BOOK isn't. I am assuming, since he makes no mention of the significance of this, that this is a typographical mistake. If the nonmanual question signal accompanied the entire string PRO.1 BORROW BOOK, it would be consistent with all the data presented here.

   Thompson argues that the second clause is not subordinate to the first, yet he translates it as if it were. Thompson translates (11) as 'I asked if I could borrow the book.' I have replaced that translation with what seems to be a more appropriate one.
2. I have replaced Thompson's translation of (12), 'Mark wanted to know what Asa gave Henry', with what seems to be a more appropriate one.

Restrictive Relative Clauses

5.0. INTRODUCTION

In this section restrictive relative clauses will be examined. First the theoretical framework in which relative clauses in English have been analyzed will be briefly discussed, and then restrictive relative clauses in Diegueño will be illustrated. This will help make clear the distinction between external-head relative clauses and internal-head relative clauses. In the next section, the Diegueño relative clauses, and the syntactic processes that disambiguate them, will be compared to ASL restrictive relative clauses and the ASL syntactic processes which disambiguate them. The two languages will be shown to be strikingly similar in both areas.

The function of a restrictive relative clause is to narrow (i.e. restrict) the set of elements described by the noun-phrase head of the relative clause. The following example is typical:

(1) The book which I bought yesterday was expensive.

The relative clause, 'which I bought yesterday', is introduced by the relative pronoun 'which' and has an external head, 'the book'. In (1) the set of books has been narrowed to one − the one I bought yesterday.

This type of relative clause has generally been analyzed in a way which reflects the fact that it has an external head. Examples (2)–(4) illustrate three such analyses. The most direct way of capturing the notion of 'head noun' involves embedding the relative clause in the determiner of a noun phrase. This kind of structure is discussed in Smith (1964), Chomsky (1965), and Stockwell et al. (1973).

(2)

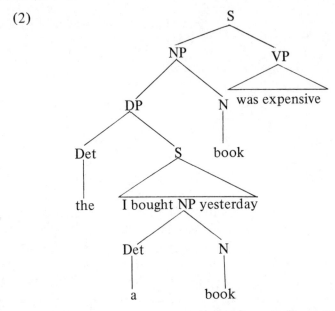

This construction makes the claim that the function of a relative clause is related to the function of other elements in the determiner. Alternatively, the following type of analysis is found in Ross (1967):

(3)

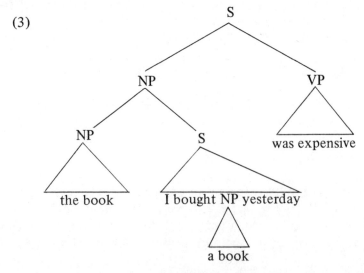

A third alternative proposed by Stockwell et al. (1973), which they call the NOM-S analysis, looks like the following:

(4)

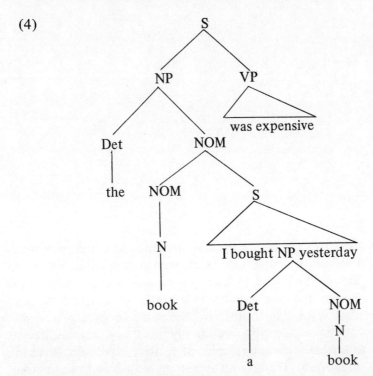

Each of the three possibilities has its strong and weak points, and exactly which structure best characterizes relativization in English is far from clear. However, they all have one thing in common: the noun 'book' appears twice in each structure. This type of analysis works well for those languages which have surface structures in which the head noun appears (also) outside of the relative clause itself (i.e. English).

Some languages, however, do not have this type of relative clause structure. Instead the 'semantic head' of the relative clause appears only inside the relative clause — even in surface structure.

This type of structure is found in several different languages. Bird (1968) analyzed internal-head relative clauses in Bambara, a West African language. Hale and Platero (1974) analyzed Navajo relative clauses of this type, Gorbet (1974) analyzed Diegueño internal-head relative clauses, and Li and Thompson (1976) analyzed internal-head relative clauses in Wappo. Fauconnier

(1971) proposed the following underlying structure for languages of this type (i.e. those with internal-head relative clauses):

(5)

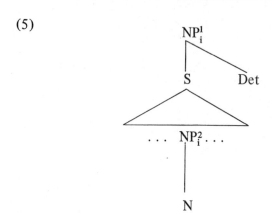

In this structure the head appears only once *in underlying structure* and is not external to the clause. In this formalism noun phrases are marked with indexes to express coreference. In the above diagram the two noun-phrase nodes are marked as being coreferential since they both have the same index (i.e. the subscript 'i'). The superscripts are simply used as a naming device. In the following section examples of relative clauses in Diegueño will be presented. The examples are presented for two reasons. First, they illustrate internal-head relative clauses. Second, the processes that disambiguate the Diegueño relative clauses are nearly the same as some of the processes that disambiguate relative clauses in ASL.

5.1. RELATIVE CLAUSES IN DIEGUEÑO

Diegueño is a Yuman language spoken today in San Diego County (California) and the northern part of Baja California (Mexico). The examples in (6) on the next page are from Gorbet (1974).

Diegueño distinguishes the clause 'i:pac 'wu:w', which can function as a relative clause, from the same string with purely sentential function, by the addition of the demonstrative morpheme 'pu' (cf. (7) on next page).

(6)

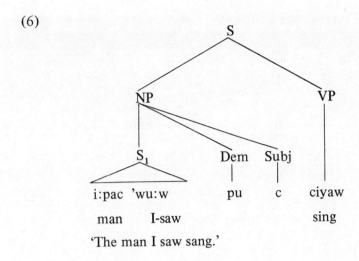

'The man I saw sang.'

(7) a. i:pac 'wu:w   [I saw the man]$_S$
     b. i:pac 'wu:w pu [[The man I saw]$_S$]$_{NP}$

It is clear that word order is not serving to distinguish a main clause from a relative clause. The normal word order in Diegueño is subject–object–verb. The order in (6) and (7) is object–verb.[1] The difference in interpretation between (7a) and (7b) is due to the presence of the demonstrative morpheme 'pu'.

Further, if a noun phrase is functioning as the subject of a sentence, the subject marker 'c' is added. This accounts for the presence of 'c' in (6).

'pu' is a demonstrative morpheme which attaches to nouns, making them more definite (Gorbet 1974: 11). A noun may or may not be marked with this morpheme but a relative clause *must* be marked with it. It is significant that otherwise the relative clause would be indistinguishable from an ordinary sentence.

As for determining which NP within an internal-head relative clause is the head of the clause, there is no trouble if there is only one noun phrase in the relative clause which could function as the subject of the matrix verb (as in example [6]). Ambiguity could arise if the relative clause contained more than one possible subject of the matrix verb, as in example (8) on the next page.

This structure can be interpreted as either, 'The rock I hit the dog with was black' or, 'The dog I hit with the rock was black.'

(8)   Construction I

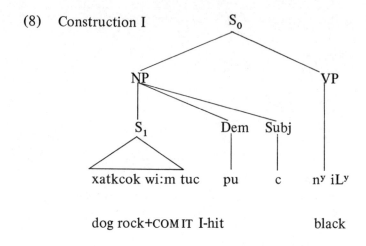

dog rock+COMIT I-hit   black

The relative clause is ambiguous because either the dog or the rock could be black and there are no structural clues to tell the listener which is being talked about. According to Gorbet, actual misunderstanding is nearly always taken care of by the context in which the discourse takes place. He states that, 'Even where more than one NP is semantically congruent, it is very likely that discourse will so clearly disambiguate that the speaker and hearer will not even notice that the sentence is theoretically ambiguous' (1974: 50).

He did, however, find two dialects of Diegueño which had syntactic devices that identify which NP in the relative clause is the internal head of the relative clause. The Mesa Grande dialect moves the head of the relative clause to a position before or at the front of the clause. Gorbet discusses the possibility that this may, in fact, now be an external-head relative clause. Within the relative clause, in place of the head, a demonstrative pronoun, 'nʸi', is left behind. This would look like Construction II (opposite page). This structure is unambiguous.

(9)   Construction II

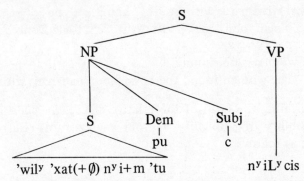

'The rock I hit the dog with was black.'

The Imperial Valley dialect has two devices that disambiguate relative clauses. The first construction simply attaches a demonstrative pronoun, 'nʸi', to the internal head:

(10)   Construction III

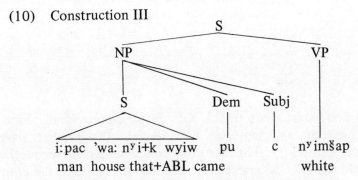

'The house that the man came from was white.'

Since 'wa: [house] is marked by the pronoun 'nʸi', it is interpreted as the head of the relative clause.[2]

The final device for disambiguating Diegueño relative clauses involves copying the head in final position in the relative clause and attaching a demonstrative pronoun to it:

(11)   Construction IV
$[[[[i:pac\ a:k\ wi:m\ tuc]_S]_{NP}\ pu\ a:k]_{NP}pu]_{NP}$
   man bone rock+COMIT hit Dem bone Dem
si:n^y+c wyaw
woman+Subj found
'The woman found the bone that the man hit with a rock.'

By repeating the head of the relative clause, the speaker avoids any possibility of ambiguity. Gorbet analyzes this relative-clause structure as follows:

(12)

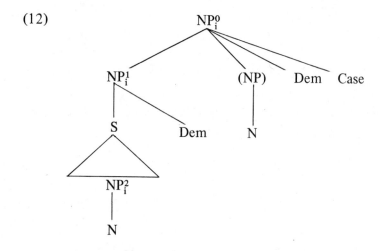

The first constituent under NP_i^0 is an internal-head relative clause; exactly the same as that seen in (8). Gorbet leaves open the possibility that the next constituent may be another noun phrase. If it is analyzed as a noun phrase, then the entire structure consists of two conjoined noun phrases with the NP node that dominates them marked by 'Dem' and a case marker.

Alternatively, without that NP node, the structure would not be analyzed as conjoined noun phrases, but as an internal-head relative clause followed by a noun, and appropriate markings.

The problem in both analyses is to explain the double 'Dem' marking. Why are both the embedded clause and the repeated noun marked with 'Dem'? This will be discussed in more detail in 5.2.8.

5.2. RELATIVE CLAUSES IN ASL

5.2.1. Introduction

Before proceeding with examples of relative clauses in ASL we will briefly review the characteristics of an internal-head relative clause in general:

(13)   a. It has a sentential construction.
       b. It functions as a noun phrase by filling a position in the matrix sentence that a simple noun phrase would fill.
       c. The relative clause is interpreted as though one of the noun phrases within it, rather than the entire clause, were filling the position mentioned in (b).

These characteristics are illustrated in the following:

(14)

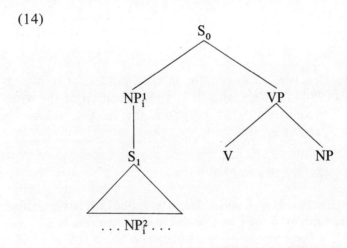

In this case the relative clause has a sentential construction (S_1). It functions as a noun phrase by functioning as the subject in S_0. Finally, the relative clause is interpreted as though NP_i^2 were filling the subject position of S_0. This third characteristic is important because it distinguishes a relative clause from a complement clause:

(15)   a. The boy *who came home* bothers me.
       b. *That the boy came home* bothers me.

The italicized portion of (15a) is a relative clause; however, the italicized portion of (15b) is not an example of a relative clause because it does not meet the condition mentioned in (13c). It is not 'the boy' that bothers me, it is 'that he came home' that bothers me. It is all of S_1 that bothers me, not just part of it.

Reduced to its essentials, an internal-head relative clause has the following form:

(16)

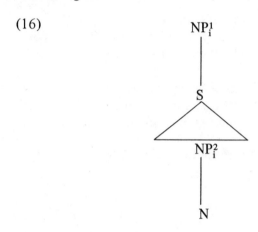

This is the structure proposed for internal-head relative clauses by Gorbet (1974) for Diegueño. It is a modification of the structure that Fauconnier (1971) proposed for relative clauses in Navajo, Hopi, and Diegueño.

5.2.2. Basic ASL relative clauses

The above structure is well suited for internal-head relative clauses in ASL. The simplest type corresponds to Construction I.

<pre>
                                    r
(17)   RECENTLY DOG CHASE CAT COME HOME
       'The dog which recently chased the cat came home.'
</pre>

The constituent structure of (17) is shown in (18).

The bar over the string RECENTLY DOG CHASE CAT in (17) indicates that these signs are accompanied by the signal 'r', seen in Plate 28. This signal serves to distinguish the same sequence of signs from the sentence, 'Recently the dog chased the cat', which would be transcribed:

(18)

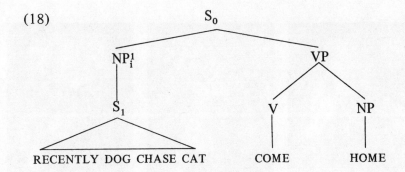

(19)   RECENTLY DOG CHASE CAT

In spite of the fact that the six pictures each show a different postural-facial expression, there are some parts of the expression which remain constant throughout the relative clause, then change at the end of the relative clause. First, the head is tilted back for the signs RECENTLY, DOG, CHASE, and CAT, but it is lowered for the signs COME and HOME. Second, the eyebrows are raised during the relative clause and lowered for the rest of the sentence. Third, the muscles which raise the upper lip are tensed during the relative clause. This gives a characteristic shape to the crease in the skin which runs from the sides of the mouth to the sides of the nose. These three independent features of the facial expression and head position, taken together, distinguish a simple sentence from a relative clause. Notice that this way of marking the relative clause is clearly not related to the individual signs contained in the relative clause. The three factors discussed above remain throughout the relative clause.[3]

There are also characteristic facial expressions associated with certain lexical items in ASL. If one of these signs occurs inside a relative clause, the one type of facial signal does not suppress the other. Rather, the effect is similar to adding the two expressions together (cf. RECENTLY in Plate 28). It seems then that the nonmanual aspects of certain lexical items, expressions associated with individual signs or compounds, and nonmanual grammatical markers are independent and additive. In fact, this appears to be a general characteristic of all the categories of nonmanual signals discussed here.

The nonmanual signal marking relative clauses was by no means obvious upon first examination of the videotapes containing them.

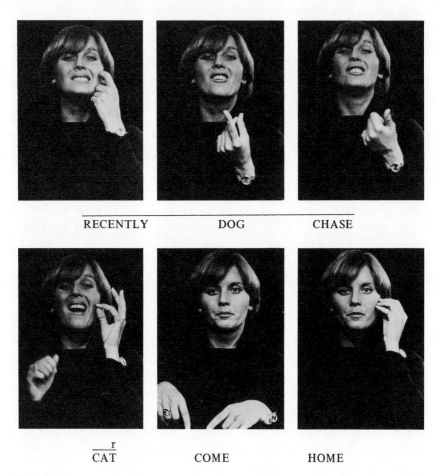

RECENTLY   DOG   CHASE

$\overline{\text{CAT}}^{\text{r}}$ COME   HOME

Plate 28.

Only when photographs taken from the television screen as the individual signs in the sentences were being made were placed side by side did it become clear that the signs within the relative clauses have those special features in common.[4]

Signers consistently interpret clauses accompanied by this non-manual signal as being used to identify one of the noun phrases inside the clause. This is not to say that a signer will always choose the relative clause construction where an English speaker would use a relative clause; there is, of course, more than one way to say the same thing. A signer could easily convey the same information using two sentences instead of one complex one.

There is also evidence that this construction is widespread. The backgrounds of the native signers who were informants for this research are quite varied. The deaf researchers at the Salk Institute are from Texas, California, Oregon, and Indiana. I was also able to consult some of the faculty and staff (hearing and deaf) at California State University, Northridge, who learned ASL as a native language, and they were in agreement as to the function of the relative clause as well as to the form of the relative clause. This work was also discussed with a research group from the Research Development and Demonstration Center in Education of Handicapped Children, which is located in Minneapolis, Minnesota, who have subsequently found results identical to those presented here (personal communication).[5]

Sentences containing ASL relative clauses were elicited by asking native signers to translate into ASL a list of English sentences containing restrictive relative clauses. To minimize the possibility that the translation might be somehow biased by the fact that the English sentences contained relative clauses, the informants were not asked for on-the-spot translations, but were given a few days. Relative clauses were not always produced. Sometimes a signer introduced information in one sentence and referred to it in the next. This seems to occur naturally if the speaker assumes that the addressee is unfamiliar with the subject. For instance, for one native signer, not involved in the above translation, a hypothetical situation was established in which there had recently been two men in the room with us, one who knew ASL and one who knew nothing about ASL, with locations established for each one. When asked to explain that the man who knew nothing about ASL knew her mother (a relative clause was not used in the request), the signer repeated the description of the situation, including establishing a location for each man, and referred to the man by referring to 'his' location. However, when asked to omit the explanation of the backgrounds of the two men and simply indicate which man knew her mother, the signer immediately produced a sentence containing a relative clause:

(20) $\overline{\text{ONE CAN'T SIGN}}^{\text{r}}$ KNOW POSS.1 MOTHER
'The one who can't sign knows my mother.'

In this case there was no translation involved; the relative clause occurred naturally and only after it was established that the previous situation was already known by the signer's addressee (i.e. two men, one who could sign and one who couldn't, had been in the room).

I also attempted to see if these relative clauses occurred naturally in stories. In one short story the amount of information concerning the three characters was carefully limited; they were not given names but were introduced as 'one man', 'another man', etc. Later in the story these characters needed to be referred to, and the most convenient way to do this in English was by using a relative–clause construction. The story was given to signers to read, and, after they were familiar with the story, each signer was asked to tell the story in ASL.[6] In their videotaped signed stories, the signers used two main ways of identifying characters. One was to assign a 'number' to each character as he was introduced; that is, the first man introduced in the story was called 'the first', which the signer indicated by touching the thumb and then signing MAN. The second man was referred to on the index finger, etc.

The other way used to refer to the characters in the story was to identify them by what they had done. This involved the use of relative clauses. For example, to identify the man who had made a beet pie, one signer said,

$$\overline{\text{(21)   MAN MAKE RED PIE}}^{\text{r}} \text{ FLIRT}^{[+]} \text{ FINISH}$$

(21) $\overline{\text{MAN MAKE RED PIE}}$ FLIRT[+] FINISH
        'The man who made the "beet" pie stopped flirting.'

Two separate studies bear upon the arbitrariness and the salience of facial expression as a grammatical signal for relative clauses. Part of the first study (Liddell 1978a) involved showing sentences containing relative clauses to hearing people studying ASL and asking them for a written translation of what they saw. There were more than 100 subjects from beginning to advanced classes. Where facial expression was the only signal for relativization, there was not one single translation which contained a relative clause. This demonstrates the arbitrariness of the non-manual signal which marks relative clauses.

A group of deaf signers was involved in another study which demonstrates the salience of the signal. Tweney et al. (to appear) conducted a sentence-perception experiment involving the perception of ASL sentences masked with 'visual noise'. This 'noise' made the task of even recognizing individual signs difficult, which, in turn, made the task of understanding the sentences difficult. Some of the sentences used in this experiment contained relative-clause constructions. Relative clauses in ASL do not use relative pronouns like 'who' in English. Though many signers will use WHO as a relative pronoun, the deaf researchers I have discussed this with regard this as an intrusion of English. None of the sentences used in the sentence-perception experiment contained the sign WHO, yet two of the subjects reported seeing the sign – in each case, in response to a sentence containing a clause marked by the 'r' nonmanual signal. One of the cases was especially interesting. The signer correctly identified every sign in the main clause but incorrectly identified every sign in the subordinate clause. In spite of this, the signer knew there was a relative clause present and actually reported seeing the sign WHO.

So far, no justification has been provided for the claim that what is being described is really a relative clause in terms of syntactic structure, and not a separate independent clause. That is,

why not assume that $\overline{\text{RECENTLY DOG CHASE CAT}}^{\text{r}}$ COME HOME

is simply a case of adjacent sentences with the subject of the second sentence deleted because it is understood, as in the diagram below:[7]

(22)

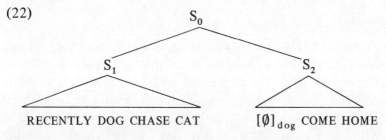

RECENTLY DOG CHASE CAT $[\emptyset]_{dog}$ COME HOME

While (22) illustrates a very common phenomenon in ASL, it is distinct from the relative clauses described here. Plate 29 illustrates the same sequence of signs signed as two sentences.

It can be clearly seen by comparing Plate 28 and Plate 29 that there is a formational difference between the two. The rela-

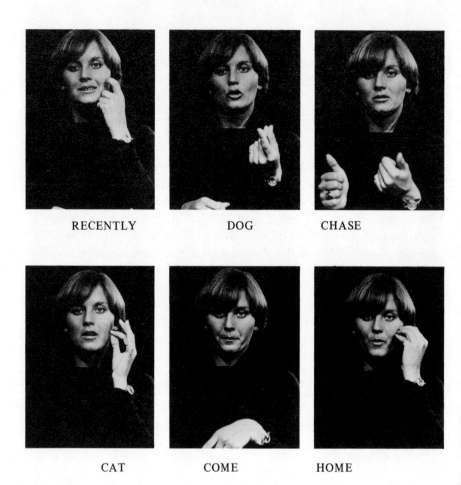

| RECENTLY | DOG | CHASE |

| CAT | COME | HOME |

Plate 29.

tive clause has a special facial expression and head position associated with it. Connected with this difference in form is a difference in what the two mean and how they behave syntactically. The two-sentence version involves two assertions. In the case of Plate 29 it is asserted that the dog chased the cat and also that the dog came home. In the case of the sentence containing the relative clause there is only one assertion — that the dog came home. It is assumed as already known that the dog chased the cat. As a result the two-sentence version is interpreted as describing a sequence of events while the sentence containing the relative clause is interpreted as describing a single event.

The sentence containing the relative clause and the corresponding two sentences also differ with respect to continuity. A break in the signing may quite naturally occur between separate sentences. By this I mean a brief relaxation of the hands other than a normal transition from one sign to the next. I have found no such lack of continuity between the relative clause and the main clause on the videotapes I have examined. What I have found is that the duration of the final sign in the relative clause is generally longer than if the same sign were to occur in either noninitial or nonfinal position. Associated with this extension in the signing time is a continuation of the nonmanual signal 'r'. When the nonmanual signal 'r' ends, there is an immediate transition to the following sign with no pause in between.

The relationship between the following times for the sign CAT are typical of the changes in duration of other signs I have timed when they occur within a relative clause. Recall that a sign like CAT, when viewed on videotape field by field, has a fairly clear 'beginning'. That is, the hand approaching the head slows down so that there is no longer a blur on the frame and the F handshape is also definite before the hand makes contact with the head. I take this to be the beginning of the sign. I count any change away from the F handshape to mean that the sign is over. I found the duration of the sign CAT to be shortest when it was neither initial nor final in the relative clause. There the average duration of the sign was 14 fields or 0.23 seconds. When CAT appears in final position the average is 24 fields or 0.4 seconds. In initial position the average is 20 fields or 0.33 seconds. In all cases where CAT appeared in initial position in the relative clause it was the logical object of a transitive verb and preceded both the subject and the verb. Not only did I find differences in duration based on position in relative clauses, there were also differences based on whether or not a given sign was the 'head' of the relative clause (methods for distinguishing the head of a relative clause are discussed later). When the sign DOG (logical subject of a transitive verb) appeared in initial position in a relative clause and was the head of the relative clause, I found an average duration of 27 fields (0.45 seconds), but if it was not the head of the relative clause the duration was 17 fields (0.28 seconds). Similarly in medial position, if DOG was the head of the relative clause the duration was 22 fields (0.37 seconds) as opposed to 14 fields (0.23 seconds) if DOG was not the head.

The duration of a sign in a relative clause is obviously a very complicated matter which appears to be affected by at least two separate factors: the position and the syntactic function of the sign.

Earlier we saw similar results where relative clauses were not involved. In comparison with medial position, signs which were topics were held roughly 22 fields (0.37 seconds) longer; initial nontopics were held 11 fields (0.18 seconds) longer; and final signs roughly 17 fields (0.28 seconds) longer.[8]

Both sets of figures were derived from limited data samples. For example, the relative-clause averages for CAT and DOG were based on 35 occurrences of the sign CAT and 31 occurrences of the sign DOG. In addition, there was considerable variation within groups which were averaged. As a result it seems reasonable to view the figures presented here as no more than tendencies.

There are further grammatical differences between conjoined sentences and a sentence containing an 'r' clause. Adjacent sentences may be conjoined with a sign like BUT, but an 'r' marked clause and a sentence cannot be conjoined in this way.

(23)   [RECENTLY DOG CHASE CAT] BUT [NOT-YET COME HOME]
'The dog recently chased the cat but hasn't come home.'

(24)   * $\overline{\text{[RECENTLY DOG CHASE CAT]}}^{\text{r}}_{NP}$ BUT [NOT-YET COME HOME]$_S$[9]
'The dog which recently chased the cat but hasn't come home.'

While there are several possible explanations for the ungrammaticality, the fact that the second sentence — with the special posture and muscular action of the face discussed above — is ungrammatical is predicted by the relative-clause analysis. It would be ungrammatical for the same reason that a sentence with a simple noun phrase subject would be ungrammatical if it were followed by BUT:

(25)   * [DOG]$_{NP}$ BUT NOT-YET COME HOME
'The dog but hasn't yet come home.'

Relative clauses may also be introduced by signs like RE-MEMBER:

(26) [REMEMBER CAT DOG BITE $]_S]_{NP}$ RUN-AWAY
      '[Remember] the cat the dog bit, [it] ran away.'

The translation looks like a question followed by a statement, but the ASL will not be analyzed in this way for the following reasons. First, the string REMEMBER CAT DOG BITE is not the same as a question about whether or not someone remembers the incident. A question about the incident would have subject–verb–object order, not object–subject–verb order.

(27) REMEMBER DOG BITE CAT
      'Do you remember that the dog bit the cat?'

Secondly, a question in ASL has its own special nonmanual signal, 'q', illustrated in Plate 30.

Third, as was mentioned earlier, a question in ASL may optionally be followed by the question marker (the finger drawing a question mark and adding a dot with a stab). It is significant that while the question REMEMBER DOG BITE CAT can be followed by the question marker, the relative clause cannot.

Fourth, a question in ASL can be preceded with the sign NOT. This forms a negative question:

(28) NOT REMEMBER DOG BITE CAT
      'Don't you remember that the dog bit the cat?'

However, the relative clause may not begin with NOT REMEMBER. This would be completely ungrammatical.

Thus there are formational, semantic, and syntactic differences in ASL between relative clauses and simple sentences or questions.

I am also assuming that the string REMEMBER DOG CHASE CAT is itself a relative clause rather than a sentence containing the main-clause verb REMEMBER, with a relative clause, DOG CHASE CAT, as its object. This assumption was made because of the presence

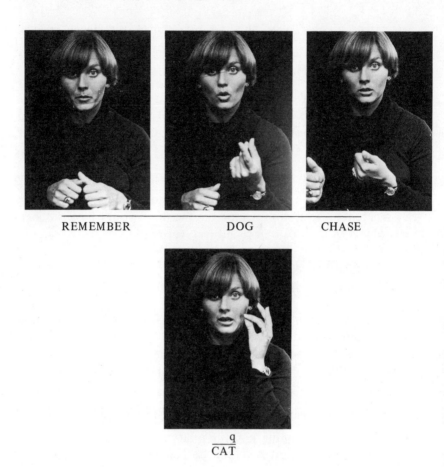

REMEMBER   DOG   CHASE

q
―――
CAT

Plate 30.

of the 'r' signal during the sign REMEMBER. According to
our analysis, if REMEMBER were not part of the relative clause,
it should not be accompanied by the nonmanual signal 'r'. If
this assumption is correct, this automatically explains why the
relative clause may not begin with the signs NOT REMEMBER.
If REMEMBER were functioning as a main-clause verb in a
sentence with a relative-clause object, then it should be possible to negate that verb with the sign NOT. If REMEMBER
is some sort of relativizer, there is no reason to expect NOT
to be able to precede it. This is the analysis that will be tentatively adopted here. If this is correct, then REMEMBER, as
a relativizer, is in some sort of middle ground because it still

has some semantic content (i.e. remembering) in addition to its syntactic relativizing function.

In all the examples presented so far, the relative clause has been in initial position. This seems to be the preferred position for these constructions. This is consistent with what was seen in Chapter 3 when topicalization was examined. Old information (i.e. information shared by the signer and the addressee) tends to be mentioned first. While the preferred position for the relative clauses appears to be initial position, they can also appear in medial and final position. The following two examples are discussed later in another context as (30) and (33). I will mention them here to illustrate that these relative clauses can appear in positions within a clause where a simple noun phrase could also appear (i.e. as the object of a verb).

(30)   PRO.1 FORCE [[BOY THATa EAT POSS.1

$\overline{\text{HAMBURGER}}$]$_S$]$_{NP}$ GIVE$^{[X:\ pro.1]}$ ONE-DOLLAR

'I forced the boy who ate my hamburger to give me a dollar.'
(The sign THATa will be discussed in 5.2.3)

(33)   PRO.1 FEED [[$\overline{\text{DOG BITE CAT THATb}}$]$_S$]$_{NP}$ THATc]$_{NP}$

'I fed the cat that the dog bit.'
'I fed the dog that bit the cat.'
(The signs THATb and THATc and the notation 'i' are
     discussed in 5.2.4)

5.2.3. THATa

During my research on relativization in ASL it became obvious that the various signs which are generally glossed into English as THAT needed to be distinguished in terms of their form. What I am calling THATa is not the same as THATb, etc. It is hoped that this notation will simplify, rather than complicate, the descriptions that follow. The signs discussed will be illustrated as they occur.

To make this sign, the forearm is elevated roughly sixty degrees above horizontal and the sign is made with a single short forward motion of the hand by bending the wrist, as shown in Figure 1. This may be accompanied by some forward downward forearm

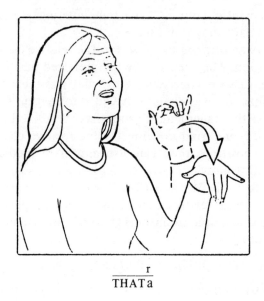

$$\overline{\text{THAT a}}^{\text{r}}$$

Figure 1.

motion. The following example illustrates its use:

(29) $[\,[\overline{\text{RECENTLY DOG THATa CHASE CAT}}^{\text{r}}]_{S_1}]_{NP}$ COME
HOME
'The dog which recently chased the cat came home.'

THATa seems to mark the entire clause S_1 as subordinate, not just the part of the clause which follows it. In other words DOG, as the above bracketing indicates, is part of the relative clause. It is not an external head. As a result DOG is not necessarily the head of the relative clause, though that is the most likely reading of (29). The processes which affect this will be discussed later.

There are times when the presence of the relative conjunction appears to prevent ambiguity:

(30)   a. PRO.1 FORCE $[\,[\overline{\text{BOY EAT POSS.1 HAMBURGER}}^{\text{r}}]_{S}]_{NP}$

GIVE$^{[X\,:\,\text{pro.1}]}$ ONE-DOLLAR

b. PRO.1 FORCE [[BOY THATa EAT POSS.1

HAMBURGER]$_S$]$_{NP}$ GIVE$^{[X:\ pro.1]}$ ONE-DOLLAR

'I forced the boy who ate my hamburger to give me a dollar.'

In (30a) THATa is not present, which could lead to confusion since the first two signs and the relative clause might be misunderstood as (31), in spite of the change to the nonmanual signal 'r' beginning with the sign BOY.

(31)   I forced the boy to eat my hamburger.

This is not a problem in (30b) since THATa is present. If the relative clause is topicalized, the reading (31) is no longer possible and the absence of THATa no longer results in a potentially ambiguous sequence of signs.

(32)   [[BOY EAT POSS.1 HAMBURGER]$_S$]$_{NP}$ PRO.1

FORCE GIVE$^{[X:\ pro.1]}$ ONE-DOLLAR

'The boy who ate my hamburger, I forced him to give me a dollar.'

The reader may be wondering why there is no indication of the nonmanual signal 't' also accompanying the topicalized relative clause in (32). The answer can be seen by comparing the nonmanual components of each signal. Recall that the signal 't' consists of these two nonmanual behaviors:

$$\begin{bmatrix} \text{brow raise} \\ \text{slight backward head tilt} \end{bmatrix}$$

The signal 'r', on the other hand, consists of the following three behaviors:

$$\begin{bmatrix} \text{brow raise} \\ \text{backward head tilt} \\ \text{upper lip raised} \end{bmatrix}$$

It is now easy to see that if the 'r' marking is present, it is impossible to know if the 't' marking is also present independently.

5.2.4. THATb and THATc

Two other signs generally glossed as 'that' play an important role in the relative clauses of ASL. They are the signs THATb and THATc. Their use is illustrated in the following example:

$$\text{(33)} \quad \text{PRO.1 FEED } [[\overline{\text{DOG BITE CAT THATb}}]_S \ \text{THATc}]_{NP}$$

with the notation $\overline{i}$ above THATb and $\overline{r}$ above the relative clause

'I fed the dog that bit the cat.'
'I fed the cat that the dog bit.'

The notation '_____i' above the sign THATb refers to an intensification of the signal 'r' during that sign. This is discussed in more detail later. Based on the criterion of cooccurrence with the nonmanual signal 'r', THATc is not part of the relative clause, though THATb is. Both signs differ in form and function from the other signs discussed in this book which have been glossed as a form of 'THAT'. These two signs are illustrated in Figure 2.

To make the sign THATb the forearm remains nearly vertical with the wrist cocked back slightly. Often there is no motion at all in this sign. However, there may be a fast but very slight shaking motion of the forearm. I have also seen this sign made by uncocking the wrist. The sign itself does not translate well. It is a sign which is made and held to give the addressee a chance to signal to the signer that he knows which person or thing the relative clause is describing. When the speaker receives such a signal (i.e. a head nod) he signs THATc.

In a context where two people have been looking for something they saw advertised, upon finding that thing, one person could point it out to the other and then sign THATc. Its meaning is very much like, 'That's the one.' THATc performs the same function in the above example. Both signers know that a dog bit a cat. THATc makes it clear that 'that's the one I'm talking about.' THATc is optional if the relative clause appears in nonfinal position. However, a relative clause may not be left hanging. If the relative clause appears in final position, either the sign THATc follows it or there is some kind of affirmative head nod which serves the same function.

THATa and THATc are similar in form but not identical. There are two significant differences: THATc begins with a backward motion, while THATa begins with a forward motion. THATc is also made with a more clear-cut end to the arm motion. That is, THATc ends with a hold and THATa does not.

There is one other aspect of (33) which is of interest. It also

$$\overline{\underset{\displaystyle\overline{}}{i}}$$

a. $\overline{\text{THAT}}\text{b}$

b. THATc

Figure 2.

provides evidence against a conjoined-sentence analysis of the data. Suppose that the conjoined sentences in (34) underlie (at some level) the surface form (35).

(34)   [PRO.1 FEED DOG]$_S$ [DOG BITE CAT]$_S$

(35)   [PRO.1 FEED $\overline{\text{[DOG BITE CAT]}}$$_S$ THATc]$_S$

In order to derive (35) from the conjoined sentence source, it would be necessary to delete *backwards* into an adjacent sentence. Not only is there no independent evidence from ASL to support such a rule, but this would violate what is believed to be a universal of human languages.

Finally, one might ask what the object of FEED is in (35). A supporter of the conjoined-sentence analysis would have to say that there is no object of FEED in surface structure.[10]

In the relative-clause analysis the answers to both of these questions are completely straightforward. The underlying structure would look like the following:

(36)

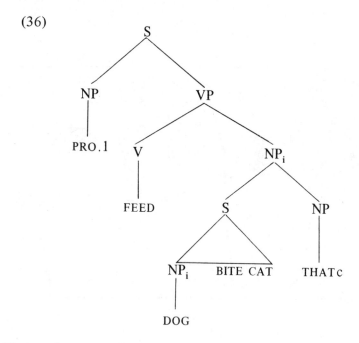

Notice that now there is no problem with deletion and there is no embarrassment about identifying the object of FEED. The object of FEED is the relative clause, and nothing has been deleted.

The following sentences are ungrammatical:

(37) a. * $\overline{\text{DOG BITE C} \overset{\text{r}}{\text{AT}}}$ ANYWAY THATc BRING HOSPITAL
'The cat the dog bit – anyway – that's the one that was brought to the hospital.'

b. * $\overline{\text{DOG BITE C} \overset{\text{r}}{\text{AT}}}$ PRO.i THINK THATc BRING HOSPITAL
'The cat the dog bit, I think that's the one that was brought to the hospital.'

They are ungrammatical because THATc has been separated from the relative clause. The ungrammaticality of these examples provides good support that THATc is not structurally equivalent to 'that's the one' in the English sentence, 'You know the cat the dog bit, well – that's the one that ran away.'

5.2.5. Potential ambiguity

ASL relative clauses have the same potential for ambiguity as the Diegueño relative clauses discussed earlier. As with the Diegueño examples, the context is usually sufficient to let the addressee know which noun phrase is to be interpreted as the head of the relative clause. Further help is provided by semantic plausibility. That is, in the following example DOG is a more likely subject of BARK than CAT.

(38) $[[\overline{\text{DOG CHASE C} \overset{\text{r}}{\text{AT}}}]_S]_{NP}$ BARK
'The dog which chased the cat barked.'

In spite of the above facts there may be times when it is desirable to eliminate potential ambiguities by some syntactic device.

5.2.6. Disambiguation without changing SVO order

Recall that the Imperial Valley dialect of Diegueño can attach a demonstrative pronoun to the noun phrase functioning as the head of the relative clause:

(10)   [[i:pac 'wa: nʸi+k wyiw]ₛ pu c]ₙₚ nʸimšap
man house that+ABL come Dem Subj white
'The house that the man came from was white.'

ASL also has relative clauses in which the demonstrative THATa (identical in form to the relative conjunction) precedes one of the noun phrases within the relative clause:

(39)   [[[THATa DOG]ₙₚRECENTLY BITE CAT]ₛ]ₙₚ COME HOME
'The dog which recently bit the cat came home.'

(40)   [[DOG RECENTLY BITE[THATa CAT]ₙₚ]ₛ]ₙₚ COME HOME
'The cat the dog recently bit came home.'

In sentences of this type the noun phrase which follows THATa is likely to be interpreted as the head of the relative clause, but it will be shown that these relative clauses are still ambiguous. It is interesting to note that if THATa is used in this way, the relative conjunction THATa does not also appear.

(41)   ? [[[DOG]ₙₚTHATa RECENTLY BITE [THATa CAT] ₙₚ]ₛ]ₙₚ COME HOME

(42)   ? [[[THATa DOG]ₙₚ THATa RECENTLY BITE CAT] ₛ]ₙₚ COME HOME

These sentences are felt to have too much in them by the informants I consulted (i.e. there are too many 'thats'). It would be premature to conclude that the relative conjunction THATa optionally attaches to one of the noun phrases in the relative clause. While this would account for the fact that only one THATa shows up in a relative clause, it ignores the fact that THATa performs different functions depending on its position.

When THATa follows a noun phrase and precedes the verb phrase (as in [29]) it is functioning as a subordinator. When THATa precedes a noun it has a demonstrative function. It refers to a previous occurrence of that noun phrase in the conversational context. For example, if a dog passes by and later someone asks about the ownership of the dog that passed by, (43) is an appropriate answer.

(43) [THATa DOG]_{NP} BELONG-TO BONNIE
'That dog belongs to Bonnie.'

There are two important points connected with THATa in the above sentence. First, no subordination is involved. This is significant because in all the ASL data I have collected, all occurrences of THATa in the frame 'NP___VP X' involve subordination. Second, the sign THAT may not substitute for THATa in its subordinating function, though some signers will sometimes use THAT as a demonstrative pronoun.

THAT

Figure 3.

Figure 3 shows the sign that beginning books on ASL refer to as 'that'. It is described in Stokoe et al. (1965: 246). This sign is associated with forms of Signed English and appears in what seem to be borrowings from English, such as THAT RIGHT ('that's right'). Some signers will accept THAT as a substitute for THATa in its demonstrative function; however, THAT is completely rejected as unacceptable when it is presented to native signers as a substitute for THATa in its subordinating function.

$$\overline{}^{\text{r}}$$

(44)   * [[DOG THAT BELONG-TO BONNIE]$_S$]$_{NP}$ BARK
    'The dog that belongs to Bonnie barked.'

The above facts suggest that there are two morphemes which are both signed THAT a, and that THAT can sometimes substitute for the demonstrative. This seems to rule out any analysis which attempts to account for the questionable status of (41) and (42) by claiming that to derive sentences like (39) and (40) THAT a (the relative conjunction) is moved to a position in front of the head of the relative clause. Since I have no alternate explanation for the questionability of (41) and (42), I will merely note the restriction that no more than one THAT a appears naturally in a single relative clause.

A second way of disambiguating relative clauses involves the use of spatial indexing. The pronoun PRO.3 (the index finger pointing) is generally, though not necessarily, used in this process. The important point is that a location in space is referred to in conjunction with the sign to be indexed. This serves to establish that location as a reference point. Later reference to that point is functionally equivalent to pronominal reference in spoken language. This type of reference has the advantage of not being ambiguous the way the pronoun 'he' is in the following English example:

(45)   When John looked at Bill he was surprised.

This sentence is ambiguous because it is not clear who was surprised — John, Bill, or someone else. This ambiguity is not present in the following ASL sentence:[11]

(46)   JOHN LOOK-AT$^{[X:\ pro.3]}$ BILL PRO.3 SURPRISE
    'When John looked at Bill he[=Bill] was surprised.'

In this example the sign JOHN is made on the right side of the signing space by the right hand. The sign LOOK-AT is made with the right hand with the extended fingers facing right-to-left with the palm down. BILL is made on the left side of the body. PRO.3 unambiguously refers to Bill because it is directed to the left. Since PRO.3 is the subject of SURPRISE, Bill is the one who was surprised.

Alternatively, if PRO.3 had pointed to the right, rather than to the left, it would have referred to John.

This process of using the signing space for indexing is the second of three optional devices that ASL has which can disambiguate a relative clause without changing the normal word order. This is illustrated in (47):

$$\overline{}\overset{r}{}$$

(47) [[DOG   BITE   CAT]$_S$]$_{NP}$ COME   HOME
    -left-   -left to   -right-   -starts on
        right-   right and moves
                         toward the body-

'The cat the dog bit came home.'

The pronoun PRO.3 is not used in this case, but the signer may take advantage of the spatial index established during the signing. By signing COME on the right, the subject is interpreted as that noun phrase which was established on the right (i.e. CAT). Note that the relative clause by itself does not indicate its head but that this is resolved by the following reference to a spatial index by the verb COME.

ASL has a third process which disambiguates the relative clause itself. It consists of intensifying the facial expression (contracting the same muscle groups more severely) and either (a) thrusting the head forward (slightly) or (b) nodding the head quickly − or both, while the head of the relative clause is signed. The intensification also raises the eyebrows even more than before. Signs which are signed with this expression will have the notation 'i' above them.

(48) [[$\overline{\text{DOG BITE CAT}}$]$_S$]$_{NP}$ COME HOME
'The cat that the dog bit came home.'

Only spatial indexing and the 'intense' marking clearly identify the head of a relative clause without a change in word order.

(49) a. THATa (relative conjunction): does not clearly iden-
        tify the head;
    b. THATa (demonstrative): does not clearly identify
        the head;

c. spatial indexing: clearly identifies the head;
d. 'intense' marking: clearly identifies the head.

In the absence of other grammatical or contextual clues for interpreting one noun phrase over another as the head of the relative clause, the noun phrase adjacent to THATa (in an S–V–O sentence) is likely to be interpreted as the head. However, this can be overridden by either spatial indexing or 'intense' marking (and also other processes discussed later).

$$\overline{}^{\ \ r}$$

(50)   [[THATa   DOG   BITE   CAT]$_S$]$_{NP}$ COME   HOME
        -left-   -left-   -left to   -right-   -starts on
                          right   right and
                                                    moves toward
                                                    the body-

'The cat which that dog bit came home.'

$$\overline{}^{\underline{\ i\ }}_{\ r}$$

(51)   [[THATa DOG BITE CAT]$_S$]$_{NP}$ COME HOME

'The cat which that dog bit came home.'

$$\overline{}^{\underline{\ i\ }}_{\ r}$$

(52)   [[DOG THATa BITE CAT]$_S$]$_{NP}$ COME HOME

'The cat which the dog bit came home.'

In (50)–(52) the only interpretation is the one shown. This is because the spatial indexing and 'intense' marking each have the ability to mark unambiguously the head of the relative clause, while the presence of THATa in either of its roles does not. If the spatial indexing and the 'intense' marking are used to identify two different noun phrases in the relative clause, the result is an ungrammatical sentence.

$$\overline{}^{\underline{\ i\ }}_{\ l}$$

(53)   *   [[DOG   BITE   CAT]$_S$]$_{NP}$ COME   HOME
            -left-   -left   -right-   -starts on left
                     to right-   and moves toward
                                             the body-

The spatial indexing marks DOG as the head of the relative clause since COME begins on the same side in which a locus for DOG was established. However, the 'intense' marking present during the sign CAT marks it as the head of the relative clause. It is not possible to interpret this sentence as meaning that they both came home. As a result, the sentence is rejected as ungrammatical.

5.2.7. Disambiguation by word-order change

Recall that the Mesa Grande dialect of Diegueño can disambiguate a relative clause by moving the head of the relative clause to a position at the beginning of the clause and leaving a pronoun behind. This process apparently applies the same way to either subject or object.

ASL also can disambiguate a relative clause by moving the head, but ASL does not leave a pronoun behind and further makes a distinction between subject and object. When an object is moved, it is moved to the left.

$$\overline{\hspace{2.5cm}}^{r}$$
(54) [[CAT DOG BITE]$_S$]$_{NP}$ COME HOME
'The cat that the dog bit came home.'

This process has the same disambiguating force as the presence of THATa. That is, both spatial indexing and the 'intense' marking will override its effect.

The process just described applies to object noun phrases, which originate on the right (i.e. after the subject and verb), and it moves them to initial position on the left. If the head of the relative clause is a subject noun phrase, which originates in initial position, some signers mark it as the head of the relative clause by moving it to the extreme right side of the relative clause. When this takes place an instance of THATa shows up before the verb. There is also a strong tendency for the moved noun phrase to be accompanied by the 'intense' marking. Notice that when this occurs the relative clause actually takes on the shape of a noun phrase: demonstrative–modifier–noun.

$$\overline{\hspace{1.5cm}}^{i}_{r}$$
(55) THATa CHASE CAT DOG RUN-AWAY[12]
'The dog that chased the cat ran away.'

This example also provides evidence against a conjoined-sentence analysis of relative clauses since the relative clause in this case does not have the form of a sentence but that of a noun phrase (i.e. $[\text{THATa BROWN DOG}]_{NP}$ RUN-AWAY). One of the original three informants who provided the data for this research found (55) to be unacceptable. However, since that time, several other informants have been consulted. They all accepted (55) as grammatical and characterized it as informal ASL signing.

5.2.8. Disambiguation by repetition of the head

Once again ASL and Diegueño have similar surface structures. Both languages have structures in which a copy of the head noun is present at the end of the relative clause and is accompanied by a demonstrative:

(11) $[[[\text{i:pac a:k wi:m tuc}]_S]_{NP}$ pu$]_{NP}$
      man bone rock+COMIT hit Dem
a:k pu$]_{NP}$ si:n^y+c wyaw
bone Dem woman+Subj found
'The woman found the bone that the man hit with the rock.'

The following ASL structure is very similar:

(56) $[[[\overline{\text{DOG BITE CAT}}]_S]_{NP}\overline{\text{THATa CAT}}^{\,r}]_{NP}$ PRO.1
    FEED$[\text{X: pro.3}]$ [13]
'I fed the cat that the dog bit.'

Both languages present exactly the same problem. Each language marks the relative clause as usual, but also attaches exactly the same marking to the repeated head of the relative clause.

In the ASL case a noun phrase follows the relative clause, suggesting that we are dealing with two conjoined noun phrases; the first a relative clause, and the second a repetition of the head. Both are marked with the 'r' signal.

However, there is no immediately apparent reason for the repeated head of the relative clause also to be marked with the 'r' signal.[14]

(57)

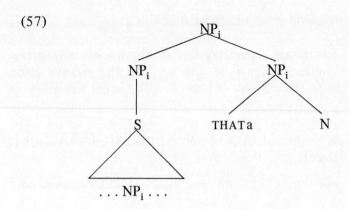

Example (56) could be further modified by preposing the noun CAT and including the 'intense' marker:

(58) $[[[\text{CAT DOG BITE}]_S]_{NP} \text{ THATa CAT}]_{NP} \text{ PRO.1}$
$\overline{r}^{\,i}$

FEED$^{[X:\ pro.3]}$

Notice that there are four separate factors functioning in (58):
  a. 'r' is present throughout the relative clause;
  b. the object, CAT, has been preposed;
  c. the head is repeated;
  d. the 'intense' marker is present during the phrase THATa CAT.
Signers consider constructions like (58) — and (56) — to be unnecessarily complicated and generally prefer to use more straightforward syntactic constructions. A sentence like the following, which has all the properties of (58) and the addition of spatial indexing, crosses the line of acceptability and is rejected as being too redundant by the signers I have consulted:

(59) * $[[[\text{CAT} \quad \text{DOG} \quad \text{BITE}]_S]_{NP} \quad \text{THATa} \quad \text{CAT}]_{NP}$
$\overline{r}^{\,i}$

         -left-   -right-   -right   -left-
                                 to left-

       PRO.1 FEED$^{[X:pro.3]}$
       -left-

5.2.9. Relative clauses with external heads

In some constructions, according to the criterion of cooccurrence with the nonmanual signal 'r', the head of the relative clause appears outside the relative clause. The following examples are typical:

(60)   ASK$^{[X:\ pro.3]}$ GIVE$^{[X:\ pro.1]}$ DOG [[$\overline{\text{URSULA KICK}}^{\text{r}}$]$_\text{S}$ THATc]$_\text{NP}$

'I asked him/her to give me the dog that Ursula kicked.'

(61)   [$\overline{\text{DOG}}^{\text{t}}$ [$\overline{\text{EAT POSS.1 HAMBURGER}}^{\text{r}}$]$_\text{S}$]$_\text{NP}$ PRO.1 BUY

'As for the dog that ate my hamburger, I bought it.'

In these two examples DOG is not signed with the 'r' signal. Instead it receives the same expression it would normally be signed with if no relative clause were present. In other words, the signal 'r' does not include the sign DOG, though it does include all the signs under the bar notation. Example (60) is illustrated in Plate 31.

The occurrence of the external head in (60) and (61) appears to be optional. That is, there are also grammatical counterparts of (60) and (61) with internal heads.

(60')   ASK$^{[X:\ pro.3]}$ GIVE$^{[X:\ pro.1]}$ [[$\overline{\text{DOG URSULA KICK}}^{\text{r}}$]$_\text{S}$ THATc]$_\text{NP}$

(61')   [[$\overline{\text{DOG EAT POSS.1 HAMBURGER}}^{\text{r}}$]$_\text{S}$]$_\text{NP}$ PRO.1 BUY

There is a strong tendency, however, for the external head to appear when the relative clause follows the verb (i.e. as in [60]).

Notice that this distinction (internal head vs. external head) is not as clear in Diegueño when the head of the relative clause precedes (the rest of) the relative clause. This is because relative clauses in Diegueño are marked only at the end of the clause, not at the beginning.

In ASL the head of the relative clause may appear not only

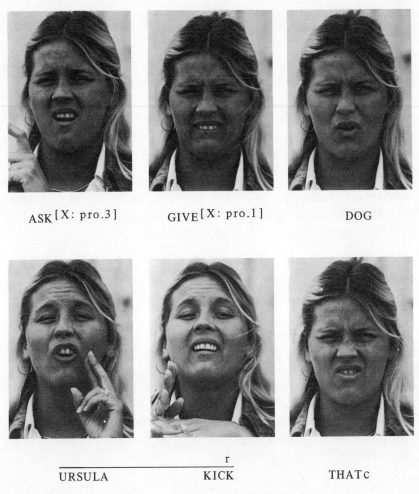

ASK [X: pro.3]   GIVE [X: pro.1]   DOG

URSULA   KICK $\overline{}^{r}$ THATc

Plate 31.

external to the relative clause but also separated from the relative clause by other constituents:

(62)   DOG BITE [X:pro.1] [[Ø CHASE CAT BEFORE $\overline{}^{r}$]$_S$ THATc]$_{NP}$

'The dog bit me, [the one] that chased the cat before.'

It appears to be the case that the relative clause has been extraposed to final position in the sentence.[15] Notice that DOG (the subject of the matrix verb and the head of the relative clause) is in the normal position for a subject and that the relative clause appears in final position with no head at all. I have found no examples of a surface structure with an extraposed relative clause in which the head is present.

(63)   a. * BITE[X: pro.1] $\overline{\text{DOG CHASE CAT BEFORE THAT}}^{\text{r}}$c

   b. * JOHN   KICK   ∅   YESTERDAY   DOG   CHASE   CAT $\underline{}^{\text{r}}$

   BEFORE THATc

Sentences like the following led to a great deal of confusion until the various 'that's were sorted out.

(64)   PRO.1 BUY CAT [[DOG BITE THATb]$_\text{S}$ THATc]$_\text{NP}$

(65)   PRO.1 BUY DOG [[THATa BITE CAT]$_\text{S}$THATc]$_\text{NP}$

In each case the head noun is external to the clause and a 'that' appears to have been left in its place. It looks like the result of a copying rule (i.e. like Left Dislocation: 'Your old skates, I threw *them* away'). This analysis was given additional support by the fact that the 'that' in (64) appears with the 'intense' signal, but I will argue here that such an analysis is mistaken. The 'that' which appears in (64) is THATb. As we saw earlier, THATb also appears when no constituents have been moved.

(66)   [[DOG BITE CAT THATb]$_\text{S}$THATc]$_\text{NP}$ CLAW[X: pro.1]

'The cat which the dog bit clawed me.'

Finally, the head of the relative clause may appear outside the relative clause without the presence of THATb.

(67)   PRO.1 BUY CAT [[DOG BITE ∅]$_\text{S}$THATc]$_\text{NP}$

'I bought the cat that the dog bit.'

On the basis of the above evidence it seems reasonable to conclude that THATb is not a pronominal copy of the head in (64). It can also be shown that no copying rule is responsible for the appearance of THATa in (65) since THATa also shows up in the internal-head relative clauses:

(68) PRO.1 BUY [[DOG THATa BITE CAT]$_S$THATc]$_{NP}$

Further, it is not always present in the external-head relative clauses:

(69) PRO.1 BUY DOG [[BITE CAT]$_S$THATc]$_{NP}$

Instead of being a pronoun copy of a moved subject NP, THATa in (65) and (68) simply appears to be the relative conjunction.

Thus, thanks to the information about constituent structure provided by the specific nonmanual signal which accompanies a relative clause, it is clear that ASL has in surface structure not only internal-head relative clauses but also external-head relative clauses. Further, in the surface form of the external-head relative clauses, no pronominal copy of the external head appears inside the relative clause.

5.2.10. Complex relative clauses

Up to this point only relative clauses involving one S node beneath a noun-phrase node have been considered. It is possible to have more complicated structures, though signers tend to use simpler structures in everyday conversation. Consider for example (70) on p. 166. This structure has three possible meanings depending on whether NP_1, NP_2, or NP_3 is coreferential with NP_i. The three possibilities (in English) are the following:

(71) I bought the cat which watched the dog eat the hamburger.
(72) I bought the dog which the cat watched eat the hamburger.
(73) I bought the hamburger which the cat watched the dog eat.

Recall from 5.2.9 that the head noun, especially if it is the object of the matrix verb, is likely to be external to the relative clause. However, with a complex relative clause like (70), an exception appears (cf. [74]–[76]).

(70)

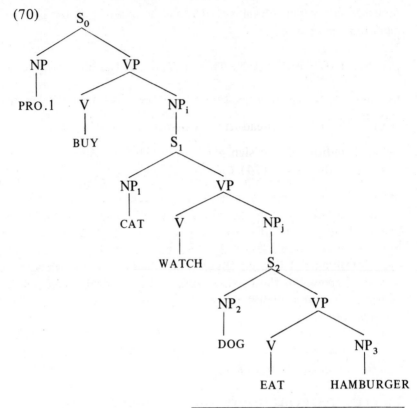

(74)   PRO.1 BUY [CAT [∅ WATCH$^{[X: \; pro.3]}$ [[DOG EAT

$\overline{\text{HAMBURGER}}$]$_{S_2}$]$_{NP_j}$]$_{S_1}$ THATc]$_{NP_i}$

‘I bought the cat which watched the dog eat a hamburger.’

(75)   ? PRO.1 BUY [DOG [CAT WATCH$^{[X: \; pro.3]}$ [[∅ EAT

$\overline{\text{HAMBURGER}}$]$_{S_2}$]$_{NP_j}$]$_{S_1}$ THATc]$_{NP_i}$

‘I bought the dog which the cat watched eat the hamburger.’

(76)   PRO.1 BUY [HAMBURGER [CAT WATCH$^{[X: \; pro.3]}$

[[DOG EAT ∅]$_{S_2}$]$_{NP_j}$]$_{S_1}$ THATc]$_{NP_i}$

‘I bought the hamburger which the cat watched the dog eat.’

Both (74) and (76) are considered grammatical but (75), though understandable, is considered odd. Before pursuing this, it is important to mention an important difference in the signing of (74) as opposed to (75) and (76). In (74) the sign CAT is made with the head facing directly forward. In (75) and (76) CAT can be signed with the same orientation which accompanies the sign WATCH$^{[X:\ pro.3]}$ (head turned to the side). This seems to be an anticipation of the sign WATCH$^{[X:\ pro.3]}$. This is significant because in the case of (74), CAT was analyzed as not being inside the clause containing the sign WATCH$^{[X:\ pro.3]}$. The fact that it is no longer influenced by WATCH$^{[X:\ pro.3]}$ provides independent support for this analysis.

The oddness of (75) may be related to the fact that it contains adjacent verbs with different subjects. This is remedied in (77) where the entire clause containing DOG is topicalized. In this example DOG also shows up in a position external to the relative clause.

(77) PRO.1 BUY [DOG [$\emptyset$ THATa EAT HAMBURGER]$_{S_2}$
[CAT WATCH$^{[X:\ pro.3]}$]$_{S_1}$ THATc]$_{NP_i}$

'I bought the dog that the cat watched eat the hamburger.'

I should also note that (77) does *not* have a reading in which the cat watched me buy the dog that ate a hamburger.

5.2.11. Underlying structures for ASL relative clauses

Any underlying structure for ASL relative clauses must be able to provide the proper framework for deriving the surface forms (78)–(82).

(78) [... [[... NP$_i$ ...]$_S$]$_{NP_i}$ ...]$_S$

In (78) the relative clause appears in a nontopicalized position in the matrix sentence without an external head. There may or may not be a copy of the head at the end of the relative clause.

(79) $[[[\ldots NP_i \ldots]_S]_{NP_i} \cdots]_S$

In (79) the relative clause appears in a topicalized position without an external head. Again, there may or may not be a copy of the head at the end of the relative clause.

(80) $[\ldots NP_i [[\ldots \emptyset \ldots]_S]_{NP_i} \cdots]_S$

This structure is like (78) but it has an external head. There cannot be a copy of the head at the end of the relative clause. This is true of all the external-head relative-clause structures.

(81) $[NP_i [[\ldots \emptyset \ldots]_S]_{NP_i} \cdots]_S$

This structure is like (79), but it has an external head.

(82) $[\ldots NP_i \ldots [[\ldots \emptyset \ldots]_S]_{NP_i}]_S$

The external head is not topicalized but is separated from the headless clause by extraposition.

From underlying structures with both an external NP head and a coreferential NP head (i.e. like examples [2]–[4]) there would be no problems in deriving structures like (80)–(82). For example:

(83)

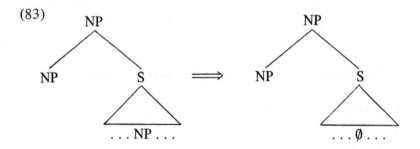

The derivations would all involve the deletion of the NP inside the relative clause. However, this analysis would run into serious difficulties with structures like (78) and (79). The difficulty stems from the deletion of the external head. The external NP bears all the primacy conditions (i.e. it both precedes and commands the internal NP) and should not be deletable on the basis of identity with the internal NP.[16] The deletion of the external NP would violate what is believed to be a universal property of human languages. That is, the controller of the deletion must bear at least one of the primacy conditions (Langacker 1966), and since the lower NP bears none of the primacy conditions, it may not control the deletion of the external NP.

On the other hand an underlying structure like Fauconnier's is ideal for the structures like (78) and (79).

(84)

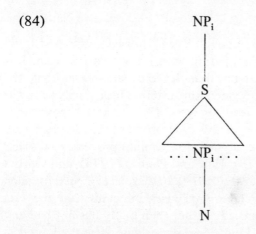

Given an underlying structure like (84), there would be no problem with the derivations for (78) and (79) because (84) is basically the structure to be derived. That is, there would be no 'derivation' since the underlying structure and the surface structure are basically the same.[17]

Deriving the external-head relative clauses from a source like (84) does not have the undesirable consequences that deriving the internal-head relative clauses from an external-head source was shown to have. What would be necessary is a rule which promotes the internal head (as shown in [85]).[18]

This would not have the undesirable consequences associated with the deletion of the external head in example (83). When the rule is applied, the result is an unambiguous surface structure.

Naturally, evidence against one solution does not count as evidence in favor of an alternate solution. This would be true only

(85)

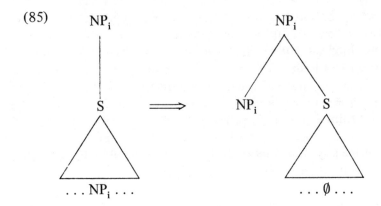

if there were exactly two possibilities. However, the ASL data *can* be used to compare competing theories of relativization. It is then possible to say that one handles the data better than the other. From this point of view, the internal-head analysis is far superior to the external-head analysis. The superior performance of the promotion analysis in this case provides independent support for those who have argued for similar processes in other languages: Schachter (1973); Hale and Platero (1974); and Gorbet (1974). At the same time, the fact that there is evidence for such an analysis in other unrelated languages indicates that the fact that ASL is produced manually rather than orally has not had any significant effect on the kind of relative-clause structures used — though the difference in mode reveals some interesting differences in the formal means of marking relative clauses.

5.3. SELF CLAUSES

5.3.1. Introduction

The sign normally glossed as HIMSELF has at least three forms and five functions. All are made with an A handshape, with the thumb extended and more or less vertical. Since ASL does not distinguish between 'himself', 'herself', and 'itself', I will refer to the third person as SELF.3.

In its basic form SELF.3 is a small sign which repeats at least once, is made near the chin, and is directed to the side — away from the signer and the addressee. One of the functions which this performs is that of a reflexive pronoun. Some may regard this use as Signed English, while others may regard this as a borrowing, and therefore part of ASL.

(86) JOHN THINK ABOUT SELF.3
'John is thinking about himself.'

The same sign also is used with a meaning parallel to the English construction, 'by himself'.

(87) JOHN SELF.3 MAKE PIE
'John made the pie by himself.'

If the sign is made larger and without repetition, we have an emphatic form of the sentence above:

(88) JOHN SELF.3[I:emph] MAKE PIE
'John made the pie all by himself.'

If the sign is made not only larger but also faster, the string has a different interpretation:

(89) JOHN SELF.3[I: ?] MAKE PIE
'Let John make the pie.'

There is a third function of the basic sign SELF.3 which we will talk about in some detail. SELF.3 apparently functions as the subject of a certain type of clause.

(90) LONG-AGO KING, SELF.3 LOVE PIE, DECIDE TAKE-UP
PIE CONTEST
'Long ago a king, who loved pies, decided to hold a pie contest.'

The clause SELF.3 LOVE PIE is either a nonrestrictive relative clause or a functional equivalent. Such clauses are signed with a different facial expression and head orientation from the clause surrounding them and different from the nonmanual signal 'r' discussed earlier. I have indicated the 'breaks' in the string by

commas. Typically, the eyebrows knit and the head is simultaneously tilted forward slightly and slightly facing to one side
(the same side that SELF.3 is directed toward). The clause is sometimes accompanied by a slow repetitive nodding of the head. The
corners of the mouth are typically pulled down and the lower lip
is tightened and (for some signers) pushed out slightly. I will
refer to such clauses as 'SELF clauses'.

5.3.2. Restrictions on SELF clauses

The most common SELF clauses involve stative predicates.

> (91)   BROTHER, SELF.3 OLD 20, EXPERT ENTER BAR
> '[My] brother, who is 20 years old, is good at getting
> into bars.'
> (⌒between two signs indicates that they are signed
> as a compound.)

As the following example demonstrates, the SELF clause can also
occur as a separate clause:

> (92)   PRO.1 SEE GIRL YESTERDAY. SELF.3 BEAUTIFUL.
> 'I saw a girl yesterday. She was beautiful.'

The following SELF clauses with active verbs are unacceptable:

> (93)   MOTHER BAWL-OUT JOHN. WHY. * SELF.3 KICK DOG
> 'Mother bawled out John. Why? He kicked the dog.'

> (94)   * JOHN, SELF.3 MAKE 3 PIE, NOT-YET CLEAN KITCHEN
> 'John, who made three pies, hasn't cleaned the kitchen
> yet.'

It would be incorrect to conclude that SELF.3 requires a stative
predicate. Active verbs may be used with SELF.3 (in SELF clauses),
but only special forms of the verb are acceptable. This requires
some explanation.

The majority of ASL verbs undergo various kinds of grammatical operations including incorporation of the location, size,

shape, and number of one or more of their arguments. They may also inflect for, among other things, continuous aspect and habitual aspect (Fischer and Gough 1974; Bellugi and Pedersen 1976). Habitual aspect is marked on the verb by a slow, drawn-out repetition of the verb with a circular motion superimposed on the basic form of the verb. Nonstative verbs which are inflected for habitual aspect seem to occur freely in SELF clauses.

(95)   JOHN, SELF.3 EAT[I: habit], ADD-ON 20 POUND
       'John, who eats a lot, put on 20 pounds.'

This example would be ungrammatical with the citation form of EAT. This poses an interesting problem. Why is this form of an active verb acceptable while the citation form is not?

The answer seems to be related to the function of the SELF clause. An examination of the acceptable SELF clauses presented so far will show that they all have one thing in common. The acceptable SELF clauses 'characterize' and the unacceptable ones do not.

Further support for this is provided by the fact that stative verbs which do not 'characterize' are not acceptable.

(96)   DOCTOR O-K JOHN NOTHING WORK. * SELF.3 SICK
       TODAY
       'The doctor ok'd John's doing no work. He is sick today.'

Apparently a temporary condition like being sick for a day does not sufficiently characterize John, and the SELF clause is unacceptable. However, if the verb SICK is inflected so that it means 'sickly', and the sign TODAY is omitted, the SELF clause is fine:

(97)   DOCTOR O-K JOHN NOTHING WORK. SELF.3
       SICK[I: 'tendency'].
       'The doctor ok'd John's doing no work. He is sickly.'

There is one other form of an active verb which is completely acceptable in a SELF clause. This is the combination of verb plus the ASL sign for 'person' (made with a B handshape) which acts as an agent nominalizer (i.e. the ASL equivalent of the English suffix '-er').

(98)   JOHN SELF.3 $\begin{Bmatrix} \text{RUN} \\ \text{DANCE} \\ \text{TEACH} \end{Bmatrix}$ PERSON

'John is a $\begin{Bmatrix} \text{runner} \\ \text{dancer} \\ \text{teacher} \end{Bmatrix}$.'

(99)   JOHN SELF.3 PERSON $\begin{Bmatrix} \text{COOK} \\ \text{WRENCH} \\ \text{PLANE} \end{Bmatrix}$

'John is a $\begin{Bmatrix} \text{cook} \\ \text{mechanic} \\ \text{carpenter} \end{Bmatrix}$.'

Whether the sign PERSON appears before the verb or after it appears to be lexically determined. It is not known what factors determine the placement of the nominalizer.

5.3.3. The structure of SELF clauses

As was mentioned earlier, there appears to be no specific non-manual signal associated with these SELF clauses which would mark them as a special syntactic construction. Further, it was shown that SELF clauses can occur as independent clauses which are not found within other clauses. This would seem to rule out analyzing the sign SELF.3 as a grammatical marker of subordination. As a result, I can see no evidence which would support analyzing these SELF clauses as some kind of nonrestrictive relative clause, in spite of the fact that they have exactly the same function.

Notice, however, that not all clauses with the same function in English are analyzed as nonrestrictive clauses either. Consider the following two English sentences:

(100)   John, who is the smartest one in the office, recommends this stock.

(101)   John, and he is the smartest one in the office, recommends this stock.

In both cases the function of the internal clause seems to be
the same: they both add information about John. The difference
is in their syntactic form. In the first case the internal clause has
a special syntactic form, a nonrestrictive relative clause. The
second example does not contain this special form. The internal
clause has the form of a sentence preceded by 'and'. Only the
first example would be analyzed as containing a nonrestrictive
relative clause. The second example contains an appositive clause.
This simply means a clause which has been 'placed' next to the
noun that it adds information about. This is exactly what appears
to be happening in the ASL SELF clauses.

5.4. CONCLUSION

The existence of the ASL relative-clause structures was noted because of the special muscular activity of the face and torso which
accompanies relative clauses. Without these nonmanual features
these structures (with the exception of those with the relative conjunction THATa) would be indistinguishable from corresponding
ASL sentences.

The relative-clause structures which were analyzed were shown
to be very similar to Diegueño internal-head relative clauses, and
the two languages were shown to have similar syntactic processes
that disambiguate the internal-head relative clauses.

In addition, ASL was shown to have a nonmanual signal that
disambiguates a relative clause − the 'intense' marker which can
accompany the head of the relative clause. If the 'r' signal does not
accompany the head of the relative clause (in initial position),
this distinguishes the entire class of relative clauses of the type
$NP[[\ldots \emptyset \ldots]_S]_{NP}$ from the relative clauses of the type
$[[NP \ldots]_S]_{NP}$. The former are unambiguous because the head
is external.

I also hope that I have shown that the fact that ASL is produced manually rather than orally has had no significant effect
on the existence and nature of the relative-clause structures used
in the language. While ASL also shares many of the same basic

grammatical processes which affect the form of the relative clauses (i.e. the movement of noun phrases, etc.), ASL also has processes like spatial indexing which are unique to a manually produced language. The specific uses of the muscles of the face and body, such as the nonmanual signal which identifies a relative clause and the 'intense' signal which identifies the head of a relative clause, are apparently unique to ASL, though the use of postural–facial expression is not restricted to a manually produced language.

Finally, the fact that ASL uses processes similar to those used by completely unrelated languages indicates that ASL is not so unusual after all. It has developed (in a very short time) in ways that parallel natural languages found in many areas of the world.

This chapter also looked at SELF clauses. Since no special marking could be found which would mark these clauses as a special syntactic form, SELF clauses were not analyzed as nonrestrictive relative clauses.

NOTES

1. The translation of 'i:pac 'wu:w' is 'man I-saw', but this does not mean that the order is O–S–V. The verb is translated as 'I-saw' because it contains the information that its subject is first person singular. If the 'I' were actually stated, it would precede the object:

   (a)   'n^{y}a: + c   i:pac 'wu:w
         I + Subj man I-saw

   Notice that the subject marker is now attached to "n^{y}a:'.
2. Margaret Langdon (personal communication) informs me that even in this dialect this process is limited to very specific grammatical contexts. As a result, this process will not necessarily be possible in any given relative clause in this dialect.
3. The fact that this nonmanual signal is claimed to be a marker for relative clauses in ASL does not imply that this is the only possible function for that signal in the language. This general characteristic of languages can be easily illustrated in the case of a spoken language like English. One way of marking relative clauses in English is with the relative pronoun 'who', as in 'The man who just walked in is my brother.' However, 'who' is also used to ask questions like, 'Who knows the answer?'.
4. Invaluable assistance in identifying the specific muscle groups responsible for producing the relative-clause facial expression which is part of 'r', and the 'intense' signal discussed later, was provided by Paul Ekman of the Langley Porter Neuropsychiatric Institute in San Francisco. The muscle groups which could be identified on our videotapes which produce the proper expression for a relative clause are muscle groups 1, 2, and 10. The reader is referred to Ekman and Friesen (1978).

   In looking at facial expressions in person, rather than on videotape, it seems to me that there is some cheek involvement in addition to muscle group 10. Charlotte Baker has provided me with information concerning muscle group 6, and it seems to describe the facial activity in the cheeks. That is, in addition to the upper lip being raised, the cheeks are also raised.

5. I have been told independently by Birgitte Bendixen, University of California, San Diego (personal communication), and Harry W. Hoemann, Bowling Green State University (personal communication), that they had the impression that the signing space is reduced during the signing of a relative clause. This appears to be true in some cases, but there are also cases where the signing space does not appear to be reduced. If the reduction of the signing space takes place, it appears to be in addition to, not instead of, the relative-clause signal discussed here. That is, reduction of the signing space by itself does not appear to be able to signal a relative clause.

In addition, when this reduction takes place the signing is often done to one side of the body rather than in the center of the neutral signing space. I have seen one signer (who learned ASL from peers at a school for the deaf) place the signing space to the side while also leaning to that side. This was during the narration of a story and may fall into the category of style. I have never seen this extreme use of space in ordinary conversation.

On the other hand, I have yet to find signers who do not interpret the combination of the nonmanual signal 'r' and the accompanying clause as being used to identify one of the noun phrases inside the clause. This is not to say that a signer will always choose the relative-clause construction where an English speaker would use a relative clause. There is more than one way to say the same thing.

6. This story is found in Appendix B.

7. The symbol $[\emptyset]_x$ will be used to point out the previous location of the deleted element 'x' in a string of signs.

8. For a discussion of the distinction between initial nontopics and topics, the reader is referred back to 3.3.

9. The '*' is used to indicate a grammatically unacceptable sentence in ASL. A '?' is used for sentences which are somewhere between fully acceptable and unacceptable.

10. In order to avoid the backward deletion and still maintain a coordinate analysis, someone might argue that it was really the second occurrence of DOG that was deleted. This would also involve a change in the surface bracketing.

a. $[\text{PRO.1 FEED DOG}]_S[\text{DOG BITE CAT}]_S$

b. $[\text{PRO.1 FEED DOG}]_S[\emptyset \text{ BITE CAT}]_S$

c. $[\text{PRO.1 FEED}[[\text{DOG BITE CAT}]_S]_{NP}]_S$

Unfortunately, this argument won't work because, as was mentioned earlier, these relative clauses are ambiguous. That is, there is one more reading to (33).

$$\overline{\text{PRO.1 FEED}[[\text{DOG BITE CAT}]_S}^{\text{r}} \text{ THATc}]_{NP}$$

'I fed the cat that the dog bit.'

It is clear that it would be necessary to delete backward. Deleting forward would give not only the wrong constituent structure but the wrong word order as well.

11. Example (46) is only meant as an illustration of one way that space and directionality can be used in ASL. In (46) John and Bill are established on opposite sides of the body by using the right hand for one and the left hand for the other. The referents could be established just as easily by leaning the body to the right and the

left and/or using the orientation of the face and eyes. In further examples, I will abbreviate the notation by simply mentioning which side the referents are established on and the direction of the verb.

Readers not familiar with ASL may wonder why (46) does not contain the sign WHEN. The answer is that although ASL has a sign WHEN, it functions only for wh-questions. In a sentence like (46) ASL relies on the order of constituents which duplicates the actual sequence of events.

12. This example is not ambiguous as to who did the chasing and who was chased. The only reading is the one in which the dog chased the cat. In other words, it is the order of the signs which indicates the grammatical relations in this case.

13. The repeated constituent is usually accompanied by the 'intense' marking.

14. The fact that in these examples the repeated head is marked in the same way that a relative clause is marked suggests that the repeated NP could be analyzed as being derived through ellipsis from (at some level) a conjoined relative-clause source.

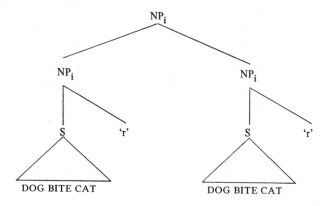

If this were the source of $\overline{[\text{DOG BITE CAT}][\text{THATa CAT}]}^{\text{r}}$, it would account for the presence of the nonmanual 'r' signal during the repeated NP since 'r' would already be present in the conjoined relative-clause source. However, the presence of THATa has to be accounted for. If a conjoined-structure analysis is appropriate for this construction, this would imply that THATa is present underlyingly as a marker of subordination, though it does not always surface. Otherwise, it would have no apparent source.

It is interesting to note that exactly the same analysis is consistent with the Diegueño data:

[[[[iːpac aːk wiːm tuc]$_S$]$_{NP}$ pu]$_{NP}$ aːk pu]$_{NP}$ ∅

    man bone rock + COMIT hit Dem bone Dem Acc

Gorbet analyzes this construction in the following way: (see diagram on next page).

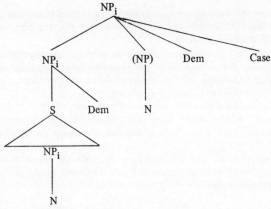

What was difficult to explain about this structure was that the relative clause marking (Dem) appeared twice: after the relative clause and after the.repeated head. In addition, there was no case marking on the relative clause. Instead, case marking appears on the repeated noun. Both these problems disappear if this data is analyzed in the same way the ASL data was analyzed.

Consider the following conjoined relative clauses.

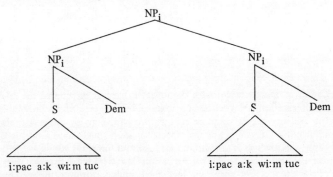

The first relative clause is marked with Dem because that is the way to mark relative clauses in Diegueño. However, in the second conjunct, a lot of ellipsis is required to derive the surface structure − only 'a:k: [bone] remains to identify the head of the previous relative clause. Because of the ellipsis 'Dem' marks a simple noun on the surface, rather than a complex one.

Finally, the fact that case marking appears on the repeated noun is automatically explained on the basis of the way Diegueño marks conjoined noun phrases for case (i.e. it marks the last conjunct). The following example shows how the first- and second-person pronouns would be conjoined and marked as subject in Diegueño:

ma: 'n^ya: + c
you me Subj   (Gorbet 1974: 27)

Unfortunately, even though this analysis accounts for the distribution of the relative-clause marking in ASL and the distribution of relative-clause marking *and* case marking in Diegueño, in exactly the same way, it relies on a theory of ellipsis which does not exist. We have simply substituted one set of problems for another: How does ellipsis work? What things can be omitted from a structure and what cannot? Why do languages have ellipsis? etc.

15. English also has a rule of relative-clause extraposition which separates the relative clause from the head of the relative clause. The following two English sentences are related by the rule of relative-clause extraposition:

   a.   A package that came all the way from Malawi just arrived.
   b.   A package just arrived that came all the way from Malawi.

16. A is said to command B if the first S node above A dominates B (i.e. it is possible to trace down the tree from the S node to B). This is discussed in detail in Langacker (1966).

   In the following tree NP_b commands NP_a since the first S node above NP_b (S_0) dominates NP_a. NP_a does not command NP_b since the first S node above NP_a (S_1) does not dominate NP_b.

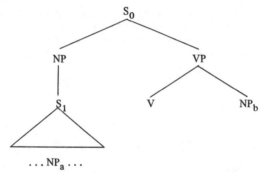

17. The derivation of the examples with the repeated head at the end of the relative clause is problematical using either an external-head source or an internal-head source. The evidence suggests that an analysis involving copying the entire relative clause and deleting everything but the repeated material might have some justification; however, this analysis is not without problems (cf. note 14).

18. Actually, on the basis of evidence currently available, whether the rule that puts the head of the relative clause under the higher NP node is a rule of promotion (as discussed in the text), or a copying rule, appears to make no difference. That is, the form of the rule could also be

since the lower NP will be deleted under coreference with the higher NP anyway.

References

Anderson, Lloyd B. (1977), 'Towards a grammar of the American Sign Language on a comparative typological basis.' Unpublished manuscript.

Back, Emmon and Robert Harms, editors (1968), *Universals in Linguistic Theory*. New York, Holt, Rinehart and Winston.

Baker, Charlotte (1976a), 'Eye-openers in American Sign Language', in *California Linguistics Association Conference Proceedings*.

— (1976b), 'What's not on the other hand in American Sign Language', in *Papers from the Twelfth Regional Meeting of the Chicago Linguistic Society*. Chicago, University of Chicago Press.

— (1977), 'Regulators and turn-taking in American Sign Language', in *On the Other Hand, New Perspectives on American Sign Language*, ed. by Lynn A. Friedman, 215–236. New York, Academic Press.

— and Carol Padden (1978), 'Focusing on the nonmanual components of American Sign Language', in *Understanding Language Through Sign Language Research*, ed. by Patricia Siple. New York, Academic Press.

Battison, Robbin (1973), 'Phonological deletion in American Sign Language', Paper presented to the 49th Annual Meeting of the Linguistic Society of America, San Diego, California (also in *Sign Language Studies* 5, 1974).

Bellugi, Ursula (1975), 'The process of compounding in American Sign Language'. Unpublished manuscript, Salk Institute.

— and Susan Fischer (1972), 'A comparison of sign language and spoken language', *Cognition* 1: 173–200.

Bellugi, Ursula and Edward S. Klima (1975a), 'Aspects of sign language and its structure', in *The Role of Speech In Language*, ed. by James F. Kavanagh, and James E. Cutting, 171–205.
– (1975b), 'Two faces of sign: iconic and abstract'. Paper presented at the Conference on Origins and Evolution of Language and Speech, New York Academy of Sciences.
– and Carlene Pedersen (1976), 'Grammatical processes in American Sign Language: modulations on adjectival signs'. Unpublished manuscript, Salk Institute.
Bendixen, Birgitte (1975), 'Eye behaviors functioning in American Sign Language'. Unpublished manuscript, Salk Institute and University of California, San Diego.
Bird, Charles S. (1968), 'Relative clauses in Bambara', *Journal of West African Languages* 5(1): 35–47.
Birdwhistell, Ray (1970), *Kinesics and Context*. Philadelphia, University of Pennsylvania Press.
Bode, Loreli (1974), Communication of agent, object, and indirect object in signed and spoken languages. *Perceptual and Motor Skills* 39: 1,151–1,158.
Bolinger, Dwight (1975), *Aspects of Language* (second edition). New York, Harcourt Brace Jovanovich.
Chomsky, Noam (1965), *Aspects of the Theory of Syntax*. Cambridge, Mass., Massachusetts Institute of Technology Press.
Coulter, Geoffrey (1975), 'American Sign Language pantomime'. Working paper, University of California, San Diego.
Crystal, David (1969), *Prosodic Systems and Intonation in English*. London, Cambridge University Press.
Davidson, Donald and Gilbert Harmon, editors (1972), *Semantics of Natural Language*. The Netherlands, Reidel.
DeMatteo, Asa (1977), 'Visual imagery and visual analogues in American Sign Language', in *On the Other Hand, New Perspectives on American Sign Language*, ed. by Lynn A. Friedman, 104–136. New York, Academic Press.
Edge, Vicki L. and Leora Herrmann (1975), 'Reversible, non-multi-directional verbs in American Sign Language'. Unpublished manuscript, University of California, Berkeley.
– (1977), 'Verbs and the determination of subject in American Sign Language', in *On the Other Hand, New Perspectives on American Sign Language*, ed. by Lynn A Friedman, 137–180. New York, Academic Press.

Ekman, Paul, Wallace V. Friesen and Phoebe Ellsworth (1972), *Emotions in the Human Face*. New York, Pergamon Press.
— and Wallace V. Friesen (1975), *Unmasking the Face*. Englewood Cliffs, N.J., Prentice-Hall.
— (1978), *Facial Action Coding System*. Palo Alto, Calif., Consulting Psychologists Press.
Fant, Louis J., Jr. (1964), *Say It with Hands*. Washington, D. C., American Annals of the Deaf.
— (1973), *Ameslan: An Introduction to American Sign Language*. Silver Spring, Md., National Association of the Deaf.
Fauconnier, Gilles (1971), 'Theoretical implications of some global phenomena in syntax'. Unpublished dissertation, University of California, San Diego.
Fillmore, Charles, J. and D. Terrence Langendoen (eds.). (1971), *Studies in Linguistic Semantics*. New York, New York: Holt, Rinehart and Winston, Inc.
Fischer, Susan A. (1973), 'Two processes of reduplication in the American Sign Language', *Foundations of Language* 9: 469–480.
— (1974), 'Sign language and linguistic universals', in *Actes du Colloque France-Allemand de Grammaire Transformationelle*, Band II: *Etudes de Semantique et Autres*, ed. by Rohrer and Ruwet, 187–204. Tubingen, Niemeyer.
— (1975), 'Influences on word-order change in American Sign Language', in *Word Order and Word Order Change*, ed. by Charles N. Li, 1–25. Austin, University of Texas Press.
— and Bonnie Gough (1974), 'Verbs in American Sign Language'. Unpublished manuscript, Salk Institute.
Friedman, Lynn A. (1974), 'On the physical manifestation of stress in American Sign Language'. Unpublished manuscript, University of California, Berkeley.
— (1975), 'Space, time, and person reference in American Sign Language', *Language* 51: 940–961.
— (1976), 'The manifestation of subject, object, and topic in American Sign Language', in *Word Order and Word Order Change*, ed. by Charles N. Li, 125–148. Austin, University of Texas Press.
—, editor (1977), *On the Other Hand, New Perspectives on American Sign Language*. New York, Academic Press.
— and Robbin Battison (1973), 'Phonological structures in American Sign Language'. NEH Grant AY-8218-73-136.

Frishberg, Nancy (1975), 'Arbitrariness and iconicity: historical change in American Sign Language', *Language* 51 (3):696–719.

– and Bonnie Gough (1973), 'Morphology in American Sign Language'. Working paper, Salk Institute.

Gorbet, Larry (1973), How to tell a head when you see one: disambiguation in Diegueño relative clauses, *Linguistic Notes from La Jolla* 5: 63–82.

– (1974), 'Relativization and complementation in Diegueño: noun phrases as nouns'. Unpublished dissertation, University of California, San Diego.

Gustafson, Gerilee (1972), *Signing Exact English*. Silver Spring, Md., National Association of the Deaf.

Hale, Kenneth and Paul Platero (1974), 'Aspects of Navajo anaphora: relativization and pronominalization', *Diné Bizaad Nánîl'iih* [Navajo Language Review] 1(1): 9–28.

Jacobs, J. A. (1859), 'The relations of written words to signs, the same as their relations to spoken words', *American Annals of the Deaf and Dumb* 11(2).

Kavanagh, James F. and James E. Cutting, editors (1975), *The Role of Speech in Language*. Cambridge, Mass., Massachusetts Institute of Technology Press.

Keep, J. R. (1871a), 'The sign language', *American Annals of the Deaf* 16: 221–234.

– (1871b), 'Natural signs – shall they be abandoned?', *American Annals of the Deaf* 16: 17–25.

Kegl, Judy A. and Ronnie B. Wilbur (1975), 'When does structure stop and style begin? Syntax, morphology, and phonology vs. stylistic variation in American Sign Language', in *Papers from the Twelfth Regional Meeting of the Chicago Linguistics Society*. Chicago: University of Chicago Press.

Klima, Edward S. (1964), 'Studies in diachronic transformational syntax'. Unpublished dissertation, Harvard University.

– (1975), 'Sound and its absence in the linguistic symbol', in *The Role of Speech in Language*, ed. by James F. Kavanagh and James E. Cutting. Cambridge, Mass., Massachusetts Institute of Technology Press.

– and Ursula Bellugi (1979), *The Signs of Language*. Cambridge, Mass., Harvard University Press.

Kuroda, S.-Y. (1966), 'English relativization and certain related problems', *Language* 44: 244–266.

— (1976), 'Pivot-independent relativization in Japanese', *Papers in Japanese Linguistics* 4: 85–96.

Lacy, Richard (1974), 'Putting some of the syntax back into semantics'. Unpublished manuscript, University of California, San Diego.

Langacker, Ronald W. (1966), 'On pronominalization and the chain of command', in *Modern Studies in English*, ed. by David A. Riebel and Sanford A. Schane, 160–186. Englewood Cliffs, N.J., Prentice-Hall.

— (1974), 'Movement rules in functional perspective', *Language* 50: 630–664.

— and Pamela Munro (1975), 'Passives and their meaning', *Language* 51: 789–830.

Li, Charles N., editor (1975), *Word Order and Word Order Change*. Austin, University of Texas Press.

—, editor (1976), *Subject and Topic*. New York, Academic Press.

— and Sandra Thompson (1976), 'Strategies for signalling grammatical relations in Wappo', in *Papers from the Twelfth Regional Meeting of the Chicago Linguistic Society*. Chicago, University of Chicago Press.

Liddell, Scott K. (1978a), 'Non-manual signals and relative clauses in American Sign Language', in *Understanding Language through Sign Language Research*, ed. by Patricia Siple. New York, Academic Press.

— (1978b), 'The acquisition of some ASL grammatical processes' Unpublished manuscript.

— (in press), 'Non-manual signals in American Sign Language', in *Proceedings of the First National Symposium on Sign Language Teaching and Research*.

Lieberman, Philip (1967), *Intonation, Perception and Language*. Cambridge, Mass., Massachusetts Institute of Technology Press.

Markowicz, Harry (1974), *Sign English: Is It Really English?* Washington, D. C., Gallaudet College, Linguistics Research Laboratory.

O'Rourke, Terrence, J. (1970), *A Basic Course in Manual Communication*. Washington, D. C., National Association of the Deaf.

Postal, Paul M. (1974), *On Raising: One Rule of English Grammar and its Theoretical Implications*. Cambridge, Mass., Massachusetts Institute of Technology Press.

Reibel, David A. and Sanford A. Schane, editors (1969), *Modern Studies in English*. Englewood Cliffs, N.J., Prentice-Hall.

Rohrer and Ruwet, editors (1974), *Actes du Colloque Franco-Allemand de Grammaire Transformationelle*, Band II: *Etudes de semantique et Autres*. Tubingen, Niemeyer.

Ross, John R. (1967), 'Constraints on variables in syntax'. Unpublished dissertation, Massachusetts Institute of Technology.

– (1972), 'Act', in *Semantics of Natural Language*, ed. by Donald Davidson and Gilbert Harmon. The Netherlands, Reidel.

Schachter, Paul (1973), 'Focus and relativization', *Language* 49: 19–46.

Sebeok, Thomas A., editor (1973), *Current Trends in Linguistics*, volume twelve.

Siple, Patricia, editor (1978), *Understanding Language Through Sign Language Research*. New York, Academic Press.

Smith, Carlotta (1964), 'Determiners and relative clauses in a generative grammar of English', *Language* 40: 37–52 (also in *Modern Studies in English*, ed. by David A. Riebel and Sanford A. Schane).

Stein, L. editor (to appear), *Proceedings of the First National Symposium on the Mental Health Needs of Deaf Adults and Children*, June, 1975.

Stockwell, Robert P., Paul Schachter and Barbara Hall Partee (1973), *The Major Syntactic Structures of English*. New York, Holt, Rinehart and Winston.

Stokoe, William C. (1960), 'Sign language structure: an outline of the visual communication system of the American deaf', *Studies in linguistics, occasional papers* 8, University of Buffalo.

– Dorothy Casterline and Carl Croneberg, (1965), *A Dictionary of American Sign Language on Linguistic Principles*. Washington, D. C., Gallaudet College Press. (Revised edition 1976, Silver Spring, Md.)

– and Robbin Battison (1975), 'Sign language, mental health, and satisfying interaction'. Paper presented at the Michael Reese Medical Center Workshop, Toward Understanding the Mental Health Needs of Deaf Adults, Chicago, Ill.

Supalla, Ted and Elissa Newport (1978), 'The form of nouns and verbs in American Sign Language', in *Understanding Language Through Sign Language Research*, ed. by Patricia Siple. New York, Academic Press.

Thompson, Henry (1977), 'The lack of subordination in American Sign Language', in *On the Other Hand, New Perspectives on American Sign Language*, ed. by Lynn A. Friedman, New York, Academic Press.

Thompson, Sandra A. (1971), 'The deep structure of relative clauses', in Fillmore and Langendoen (eds.), pp. 78–94.

Tweney, Ryan, Scott K. Liddell and Ursula Bellugi (to appear), 'The perception of grammatical boundaries in ASL', *Discourse Processes*.

Valentine, E. G. (1872), 'Shall we abandon the English order?', *American Annals of the Deaf* 17: 33–47.

Appendix A

INDEX OF THE MAJOR NONMANUAL SIGNALS

This index includes the major nonmanual signals which were found to perform syntactic functions. The columns below indicate the symbols used, the physical properties of the signal, the grammatical function performed by the signal, and a reference to a section in the text where it is discussed.

Symbol	Physical Properties	Function	Reference
'q'	brow raise head forward body forward	yes–no question marker	2.2.2 Plate 5
't'	brow raise slight backward head tilt	topic marker	2.2.4 Plate 7
'r'	brow raise backward head tilt cheek and upper lip raised	relative-clause marker	5.2 Plate 28
'n'	side-to-side headshake special facial expression	negating signal	2.3.3 Plate 9

Symbol	*Physical Properties*	*Function*	*Reference*
'hn'	[slow head nod]	assertion/ existence marker	2.3.2

'mm'	⎡lips together and
	  pushed out without
	  puckering
	slight head tilt⎤
		adverb	2.4.1
			Plate 10

'cs'	⎡shoulder raised head turned to side special facial expression⎤	adverb	2.4.2 Plate 13
'th'	⎡lips apart and pushed out tongue protruding⎤	adverb	2.4.3 Plate 15

Appendix B

"THE KING'S PIE CONTEST"

A long time ago there was a king who loved pies. He couldn't get any, because the man who usually baked pies had run away to get married to a gypsy. The king decided to have a contest. The man who could bake the best pie would be able to marry his daughter. But the news only attracted three men.

One man planned to bake a celery pie, another planned to bake a beet pie, and the last man planned to steal both pies because he didn't know how to cook.

The day of the contest finally arrived. One man put his celery pie in the oven and went outside to smoke a cigarette. The other man put his beet pie in the freezer to set and went to flirt with one of the king's servants. While the two men were gone the last man stole both the pies and took them to the king. In the meantime, the man that baked the celery pie finished his cigarette, came back inside and found his pie gone. He thought that the man who made the beet pie had stolen it. At the same time, the man who made the beet pie found that his pie was stolen too, so he thought that the man who made the celery pie had stolen it. Each of the two men started looking for the other one. The two finally met face-to-face with fire in their eyes. Just at that moment, they heard a bugle and someone announced that the contest was over. The two men looked out in the street just in time to see the king's daughter and the third man leave.

The two realized that they were both innocent. They were glad that the other man had stolen the pies because the king's daughter was so fat that it was impossible to tell if she was walking or rolling.

Index to Signs